The Heart of the

FAMILY

BOOKS BY ADRIAN PLASS

A Year at St Yorick's
Adrian Plass Classics
An Alien at St Wilfred's
And Jesus Will Be Born
Clearing Away the Rubbish
Colours of Survival (with Bridget Plass)
From Growing Up Pains to the Sacred Diary
Ghosts
The Heart of the Family
Never Mind the Reversing Ducks
Nothing but the Truth
The Sacred Diaries of Adrian, Andromeda and Leonard
Stress Family Robinson
Stress Family Robinson 2: The Birthday Party
The Visit
Why I Follow Jesus
You Say Tomato (with Paul McCusker)

The Heart of the
FAMILY

LAUGHTER *and* TEARS
from a ~~PERFECT~~ FAMILY
REAL

ADRIAN PLASS
Compiled by Bridget Plass

ZONDERVAN™

GRAND RAPIDS, MICHIGAN 49530 USA

ZONDERVAN™

The Heart of the Family
Copyright © 2003 by Adrian Plass

Requests for information should be addressed to:
Zondervan, *Grand Rapids, Michigan 49530*

Adrian Plass asserts the moral right to be identified as the author of this work.

Library of Congress Cataloging-in-Publication Data
Plass, Adrian.
   The heart of the family : laughter and tears from a real family / Adrian Plass;
compiled by Bridget Plass.
      p. cm.
   ISBN 0-007-13047-3 (hardcover)
      1. Family—Religious life—Miscellanea. 2. Plass, Adrian—Family—Miscellanea.
I. Plass, Bridget. II. Title.
BV4526.3.P58 2003
248.4—dc21   2003004966
                                                                              CIP

This edition printed on acid-free paper.

Interior design by Susan Ambs

Printed in the United States of America

03 04 05 06 07 08 09 / ❖ DC/ 10 9 8 7 6 5 4 3 2 1

This book
is dedicated to the memory
of Joseph and Mary,
the earthly parents of Jesus,
who with the following eight words
began a trend
that has continued in families
to the present day:
"Son, why have you treated us like this . . . ?"

CONTENTS

Part Four: Priorities

Part Five: Power of the Past

Part Six: Death of Loved Ones

Part Seven: The Father's Love

INTRODUCTION

Bridget and I have four children, Matt, Joe, David, and Kate, their ages ranging from twenty-eight to fifteen. We all love each other very much, but we have been through terribly negative as well as tremendously positive times in the course of the last couple of decades.

The year that is ending as I write is a very good example. Early in the month of August we received a telephone call at three o'clock in the morning to say that our twenty-three-year-old son, Joe, had fallen thirty feet from the top of some scaffolding near his home and was seriously injured. We threw our clothes on and raced to the hospital where he had been admitted, and we found him in a very bad state indeed. Joe's jaw had been broken in five places and would need thirty-eight screws to hold together the metal plates that the doctors were planning to insert. His left wrist was shattered – "destroyed" was the word that the surgeon used. His third major injury was to his left leg. The femur was snapped in two. The general trauma was very great as well. Over the next few days our son's life hung in the balance, as his body struggled to breathe for itself.

It was a terrible, emotional, frightening time. We prayed of course, and so did many of our friends. Whenever possible Bridget and I laid hands on Joe's injuries and asked God to heal him. We knew, though, that God does not always give us what we want, however clear and obvious we may feel our needs to be. People do die of their injuries, Christians as well as non-Christians, and we are not allowed to dictate any particular course of action to our heavenly Father. We just pleaded with him for this precious life and hoped against hope that he would answer our prayers in the way that suited us.

God was merciful. Our son has recovered. The surgeon said that Joe's broken jaw was the worst he had ever seen but that his work on it was the best he had ever done. The "destroyed" wrist is now functioning at a near-perfect level. The femur is healed and becoming stronger every day. Joe has a very slight difference in the length of his legs to remind him of how close he came to disaster, but with that exception he is likely to make a full recovery.

Coming so near to losing a close family member has an extraordinarily focusing effect. As a result of what happened to Joe we have all realised just how valuable we are to each other, but that is certainly not because we are a perfect family. In fact, we are very far from being perfect as a family. We are even further from being the perfect Christian family. Loving each other certainly doesn't mean that we don't spend quite a lot of time annoying each other as well.

Bearing this in mind, we, and all those other families who can identify with the rocky path we have travelled, should undoubtedly salute those who do manage to bring up those perfect Christian families that you sometimes read about. We should admire them, we should respect them, we should thank them for their example, and perhaps we should pop round tomorrow to hit a selection of them with a baseball bat, quite gently, you understand, but just hard enough to make them angry so that they sin a little bit.

I have a feeling that people who run perfect families will not appreciate this book. They would prefer one of those "how-to" books, even though they don't need one because they are perfect. One of my ongoing projects is a volume on how to build and light a bonfire that can be used to destroy most of the Christian "how-to" books that have been written on the subject of family life. They are meant to help, but they actually make many of us feel weak and foolish. This book, by contrast, will certainly not tell you how to bring up your family, but it might reassure you that most of us are making the same sort of mistakes along the way. It includes fiction, true stories, dialogues, sketches, and a little poetry, all embracing the joys, tragedies, puzzles, and problems involved in being not only part of a human family but also part of the family of God.

God bless you as you read this book. Remember that God loves your family even more than you do and that he may find them just as irritating at times.

Part One

The Problem with

PERFECTION

The main problem with being perfect is really very simple. We're not. And the chances of us achieving such a goal on this side of heaven are infinitesimal. Granted, we are made perfect and justified in the eyes of God because of the sacrifice that Jesus has made, but we still have to live with ourselves from day to day, and that can sometimes be discouraging.

Take heart! You may think that you are alone in falling so far short of the glory of God. I can assure you that you are not. Join me as we look a little further into this matter.

FAMILY
NEWSLETTER

I wrote my first *Sacred Diary* book way back in the mid-eighties. At that time nobody was quite sure which of the trappings of faith could be laughed at and which were sacrosanct. I was as confused as anyone else, but I did sense that some of the things we Christians did and said were just a little silly and, at times, even rather dangerous. The main protagonist is Adrian, a good-hearted twit who records his adventures without realising how much of himself he is actually revealing. I suppose there is quite a lot of me in this character, but I only gave him my name because the *Adrian Mole* diary books were very popular at the time, and I never realised how many people would eventually read the book and its successors. The other main characters are purely fictitious. Adrian's wife, Anne, is wise, kind, and long-suffering. Their son, Gerald, is a likeable, irreverent young man who finds much Christian behaviour far too funny to take seriously.

One of the modern plagues for members of those Christian households who do their best but fall far short of the ideal, is the yearly arrival of printed newsletters from apparently wonderful families. In one of the *Sacred Diary* books Gerald caricatures the more extreme of these intimidating epistles.

Dearest (please fill in own name),

It hardly seems possible that a whole year has passed since our last newsletter went out. What a lot has happened since then! Each of us has seen change, beginning with the youngest.

Naomi (Age 5)

Little Naomi has become more spiritually alive than ever during the last twelve months. All four of us have the stigmata now. She is also very bright, but Rebecca and I are anxious that she should not be pushed too far, too quickly where school work is concerned. She must certainly finish her reception year before taking maths "A" level, and there is absolutely no question of her undertaking piano recitals in Europe until she has passed her seventh birthday.

Naomi continues to work hard at building up the Christian union that she started at her junior school last term and is very encouraged by a recent experience of personally leading her orthodox Jewish head-master and several other members of staff (including the caretaker and three dinner-ladies) to Christ.

Naomi's after-school activities include a chess class on Monday (she earns her own pocket money by teaching that), applied thermonuclear dynamics on Tuesday, netball training with other members of the county team on Thursdays, and a soup-run into the East End every Friday evening. Typically, Naomi taught herself judo and karate to black-belt standard from text books before embarking on this poten-tially dangerous occupation.

Naomi is easily the most popular girl in her class and was voted Miss Young and Humble at church this year, although she refused to accept the trophy saying that she was an unworthy winner. This act of pure unselfishness resulted in her being nominated for the award of *Most Humble Church Member of All*, an award that she subsequently won and decided to accept, feeling that it would have been uncharitable, churlish, and subtlely vain to refuse.

Please pray with Rebecca and me that Naomi will learn how to put herself first from time to time. Failure to do this is her major fault.

Joshua (Age 16)

Joshua has gained fifteen A grade G.C.S.E.'s and nine spiritual gifts this year, including Sociology and Prophecy (the one to be most earnestly sought after, according to the apostle Paul – Prophecy, that is, not Sociology). Over the next two years he hopes to take the word of the Lord to communist China, and twelve "A" levels.

Joshua spent his summer holiday converting Guatemala with a group of pals, constructing a life-size working model of Apollo 3 out of drinking straws, and practising the five Cantonese dialects in which he is now practically fluent.

It is not all plain sailing with Joshua, however. A typically wayward and rebellious sixteen-year-old, he has several times sneaked off to his room to do a couple of hours extra academic study when he should be concentrating on tightening up his dressage skills in the back paddock ready for the Olympics, and on more than one occasion he has actually disappeared from the house altogether, only to be discovered guiltily shopping for the elderly lady who lives two doors away from us or sitting and reading to her for long periods after cooking and serving her evening meal. When Rebecca and I gently pointed out that we can't always do exactly what we want, Joshua asked our forgiveness and repointed the brickwork of every house in the street as an act of repentance. Rebecca and I feel sure he'll come through in the end.

Both Oxford and Cambridge Universities have applied to have Joshua join them in two years' time, and he will probably fly up (as soon as his pilot's licence comes through) to look over both establishments before making a decision. Please pray for Joshua's feelings of inadequacy as he prepares to deal with fellow-students and their inevitable dependency on him during this next sixth-form phase of his life.

Rebecca

Rebecca continues to enjoy producing homemade jam, bread, cakes, wine, preserves, crocheted bedspreads, small animal models made out of baked dough, dried flower decorations, knitted baby-clothes, banners and kneeling mats for our local church, and meals for the housebound.

She has completed her first novel this year, held a successful one-woman oil-painting exhibition, been awarded a third Open University degree, and continues to single-handedly look after our twelve-acre ornamental garden, when her duties as mother, wife, amateur apiarist, semi-professional photographer, local magistrate, prison visitor, hospital volunteer, leading light in the amateur dramatic association, treasurer of the ladies tennis club, district council member, and world chairperson of Women Against Poverty allow.

Rebecca is currently looking for some new challenge to occupy the spare time that she, in common with many non-working mothers, finds hanging so heavily on her hands. Next year, in addition to her present activities, she plans to become a special policewoman, stand as a prospective parliamentary candidate, complete a solo sailing trip around the world, and find a method of bottling gooseberries that doesn't lose all the flavour.

Please pray that Rebecca will develop a stronger sense of self-worth in the company of other women.

Simon

Simon has spent much of this year seeking the Lord's will for his life, and longing to serve in some more specific way. There has, however, been little space for this prayer to be answered as Simon's time has been filled with distractions throughout the twelve months, not least of which was the leading of twenty-five convoys of thirty lorries each to mid-European countries in need of aid. This took up most of the summer.

It did seem possible that the autumn would be free for Simon to concentrate on seeking guidance, but flying back from what had been an amazingly successful business trip in Hong Kong, his plane crashed into the Pacific Ocean and Simon, who was the sole survivor, swam ashore to an island inhabited by primitive natives who had never heard the gospel before. In the two months that Simon was stranded on the island he managed to learn the native tongue, devise a written version of the language, and translate a large part of the New Testament (memorised) into a form that the islanders could understand. The entire population of the island became Christians as a result, and many of them set out in canoes to take the good news to thousands of other primitive peoples living on islands in that part of the Pacific.

Simon was eventually rescued by a passing ship that was named *The Dirty Digger* when it landed at the island but had been rechristened *Redeemed* by the time it arrived at Portsmouth. Simon arrived home in the new year frustrated by these delays but as determined as ever to see if the Lord had some task that might be specially his.

In February he went into retreat in a monastery in Wales and was just beginning to feel that he was getting somewhere when, one night, the building caught fire and Simon rescued twenty-two monks whose vows of silence had prevented them from calling for help.

Simon stayed in Wales with the monks for several weeks after the fire, helping to rebuild the monastery and telling the brothers about the new life of the Spirit that was promised to all Christians. All twenty-two made fresh commitments as a result, and the Prior pledged that he would spread the good news throughout the worldwide order of which they were part.

Simon therefore returned without the leading he had sought and is hoping that next year might be the time when the Lord sees fit to give him a substantial task.

Pray that Simon will find the strength to ignore distractions from the evil one when they appear and run for the finishing line in a more decisive and intelligent way.

That's all now from this very ordinary Christian family. See you next year!

Yours,

Simon, Rebecca, Joshua, and Naomi.

P.S. We usually add a little bit at the bottom in Biro to make it more personal, but our time is the Lord's, not ours – if you see what we mean.

●—◆—●

Sacred Diary of Adrian Plass, Christian Speaker,
Aged Forty-Five and Three Quarters

KATHY AND MOTHERHOOD

The *Stress Family Robinson* books are fictional accounts of the way in which a more-or-less typical Christian English family deals with the collision between faith and real life on a day-to-day basis. As we shall be meeting the Robinsons and their family friend again in the course of this book, I might as well introduce them to you now.

Mike Robinson, a calm, kindly, but perhaps slightly unimaginative junior school headmaster, is married to Kathy, an attractive, emotional, generally well-meaning person, who explodes and crumples with rather alarming frequency. Kathy was a writer before her children came along and can't help feeling a little resentful about the way in which "family" has taken over her life.

Jack, the oldest child, is warm, witty, and almost a grown-up, though he can revert to more immature behaviour when in conflict with his younger brother Mark.

Mark is a typically self-absorbed teenager, whose life revolves around his friends and his spare-time activities. Mark's untidy, disorganised approach to life infuriates his mother on a regular basis, and there is further tension over the issue of "church", an institution for which Mark feels deep loathing.

Felicity is the youngest child, a lively, ingenuous, lover of life, who adores her brothers and deals skilfully with her parents.

"Dip", a single lady who works as a nurse at the local hospital, is almost an honorary Robinson. She is very close to all the members of the family and has a special bond with Mark.

The Robinsons are very far from perfect, but they do try hard. In this selection Kathy and Dip discuss Kathy's problems and deficiencies in her attitude towards her children. Dip is the narrator.

"Shall I tell you one of the most depressing things about being a parent?" said Kathy one blowy morning as we hung clothes out in the garden together.

I replied through a mouthful of pegs, "Only if you tell me one of the nicest things about being a parent first. Sit down there for a minute while I peg these socks up and tell me what you've enjoyed."

Kathy threw back her dark-haired head, laughed, and flopped obediently onto the dilapidated wooden bench that constituted the Robinson's "Garden Furniture". Leaning back against the trunk of the ancient apple tree that supported one end of the washing line, she closed her eyes and thought for a moment.

"I enjoyed conceiving them – and they've made me laugh as much as they've made me cry. That do?"

"Go on then, the most depressing thing about being a parent?"

She linked her fingers behind her head and closed her eyes.

"On a day like this, when the wind's whipping those sheets around, and everything's coloured like a ladybird book, I get sort of excited. I almost begin to believe I might have a present – a now – of my own. Just for a second or two I get these tantalising little nibbles and tastes of memory about how it felt to be me without constant reference to a houseful of other people. Most of the time I feel I'm living in my children's pasts. I've indefinitely postponed being myself in order to serve them, I'm out of the current of my own life, if you see what I mean. I'm not even getting wet. I might as well – "

"Cold drink, Mum?"

Jack's unexpected arrival in the garden with two tall glasses of iced orange juice and lemonade stemmed the flow temporarily. I sat down on the bench beside Kathy as she sipped ecstatically from the glass in her hand.

"What was I saying?"

"That you have indefinitely postponed being yourself in order to serve your children. Then Jack brought you a drink and you stopped."

"Yes, well doesn't that just prove my point? I'm not even allowed to feel sorry for myself without one of them deliberately doing something completely out of character and spoiling everything!"

She threw me a rueful glance.

"You must think this sounds horribly selfish but sometimes I get razor-blade close to resenting the fact that I mother around like crazy in my children's early lives, making it all happen for them, trying to give them the possibility of becoming reasonably all right, happyish adults while being fully conscious that I might fail anyway. If Mark ever becomes famous he'll write about me in the *Sunday Times* colour supplement."

Kathy moved her cupped hand through the air in front of her face, as though a double page was spread before her eyes.

"'The beginning of my life as a genuine personality was inevitably postponed until the day when I finally escaped the cyclonic context of emotional chaos that my mother created. It may have been survival but it certainly wasn't nurture' – see what I mean? Why should I change his nappies if he's going to write things like that?"

When I'd stopped laughing, I said, "Has it not occurred to you, Kathy, that your children don't actually need a good mother, which is what you're frightened you'll never be, because all they've ever really wanted – is *you*?"

●—◆—●

Stress Family Robinson

PURE JOY

What about the following quotation from the book of James? Somewhat challenging, wouldn't you say? How on earth are any of us supposed to live up to these expectations? Well, the amazing news is that my wife and I have managed it! Read the dialogue that follows the Bible passage and you'll find yourself right inside a typically triumphal incident in the lives of the Plasses.

We wish!

(This selection comes from *When You Walk*, a compilation of the comments on Bible passages that I have contributed over several years to *New Daylight*, a daily reading resource published by the Bible Reading Fellowship three times every year.)

Consider it pure joy, my brothers, whenever you face trials of many kinds, because you know the testing of your faith develops perseverance. Perseverance must finish its work so that you may be mature and complete, not lacking anything. If any of you lacks wisdom, he should ask God, who gives generously to all without finding fault, and it will be given to him. But when he asks, he must believe and not doubt, because he who doubts is like a wave of the sea, blown and tossed by the wind. That man should not think he will receive anything from the Lord; he is a double-minded man, unstable in all he does.

James 1 : 2–8

BRIDGET: (*Entering euphorically*) You'll never guess what, Adrian!

ADRIAN: (*Filled with anticipatory pleasure*) What's that then, Bridget?

BRIDGET: Well, the car won't start, and it looks as if the problem is a highly complex and expensive one.

ADRIAN: (*Clapping ecstatically*) That's really great, Bridget! Fancy that happening on the same morning that we get a huge electricity bill we can't possibly pay and the ceiling collapsing in the front room. I must say that I consider all these things pure joy, don't you?

BRIDGET: (*Almost dancing with delight*) Oh, yes! It's a wonderful opportunity for us to develop perseverance through the testing of our faith.

ADRIAN: (*With tears of sheer happiness in his eyes*) Yes, indeed! I should think we'll be as mature and complete as it's possible to be after this little lot, won't we?

BRIDGET: (*Excitedly*) Let's ask God for wisdom to deal with everything, shall we?

ADRIAN: (*Fascinated by such a novel idea*) Yes! After all, he does give generously without finding fault, doesn't he?

BRIDGET: (*Struck by yet another thought*) And let's not doubt!

ADRIAN: (*Amused at the very idea*) Oh, no, of course not, because then we would be like waves of the sea, blown and tossed by the wind. If we're like that we shouldn't expect to receive anything, should we?

(*They laugh heartily together*)

BRIDGET: (*Almost choking with merriment*) We don't want to be double-minded and unstable, do we?

(*They collapse on the floor, laughing and crying hysterically*)

•◆•

When You Walk

FAILURE

Sometimes the sense of failure really hurts, doesn't it? I wrote this poem or prayer on a day when I felt particularly useless. On that same day, however, I had happened to read those amazing words that Jesus spoke from the cross. "My God, my God, why have you forsaken me?" He was there first. The awareness of those words turned what I wrote from a moan into a sort of psalm.

This selection comes from *The Unlocking*, a book about the fears that many Christians are prey to. It was a very hard book to write because I had to tell the truth about myself.

On this particular day, I feel a failure.
What am I allowed to wonder, Father?
Am I allowed to wonder why you make it all so difficult?
Even as I say those words the guilt settles.
Perhaps it isn't really difficult at all.
Probably it's *me* that's difficult.
Probably, because of my background and my temperament
    and my circumstances, it was always going to be difficult for me.
But what if that's just a cop-out?
What if I'm kidding myself?
What if, deep inside, I know that my own deliberate doing
    and not doing has always *made* it difficult?
What if I'm one of those who has been called but not chosen?
In that case it's not difficult – it's impossible.
What if you don't exist at all and death is a sudden stumble into
    silence?
(Can you let me know if you don't exist, by the way –
    before Friday night, if it's all the same to you.)

There are moments, Father, when it's *so* easy,
    so easy that I can't remember why it ever seemed so difficult.
Those moments pass – they're valuable – but they pass.
Have you noticed how, when those moments have gone,
    I try to walk away, but I can't?
I think I shall follow you even if you don't exist.
Even if I'm not chosen.
Even if it goes on being difficult . . .
Are you still listening?
I'm sorry to have made a fuss,
It's just that, on this particular day, I feel a failure.
My feet and my hands hurt,
And there's this terrible pain in my side.

◆

The Unlocking

ROSEMARY'S LETTER

Behind all the noise and apparent confidence of upfront church activities you will always find people (we meet lots of them) who can't bring themselves to believe that God can possibly have any interest whatsoever in their spindly existence. He probably doesn't even know who they are. How can they be members of the family of God? They know the theory quite well, but so what?

This letter comes from *A Year at St Yorick's*, a book purporting to comprise a set of twelve church magazines from the totally imaginary parish of Gently Down.

Dear Father,

Forgive me for calling you that, because you probably won't even know who I am. Oh, I'm ever so sorry – saying you don't know who I am sounds as if I don't believe you're – which is the word that means you know everything? *Omniscient*, that's the word. Because I do. Believe that you are omniscient, I mean. It's just that I don't feel, well, important enough to be part of, you know, your kingdom. Oh, dear, that sounds as if I don't believe you're powerful enough to make it possible, but I do really, it's just that – oh, I'm such a – a bad person. I don't mean that I don't think Jesus died for me and all that. I do! I do! That must have sounded so ungrateful, but it wasn't supposed to, because I'm not. Sorry, I didn't put that very well did I? What I was trying to say was that I'm not ungrateful. I'm grateful – I honestly am. It's just that I don't always feel ... Well, why am I so sure that everybody else is saved and all right and everything, but I'm not? Sorry! I shouldn't have said that, should I? Christians have a lot to be joyful about, I know that, and on a very deep level I'm sure that I am – I am joyful, of course I am. But you're supposed to feel it sometimes, aren't you? Or perhaps you're not.

27

Anyway, thank you for – for – well, for all the people at St Yorick's. They're all nice. Oh, dear, that sounds bland, doesn't it? How silly. Do forgive me – well, of course you forgive me. Forgive me – I mean – I mean, well, anyway . . .

Yours Faithfully,
Rosemary.

A Year at St Yorick's

GETTING
THERE

Women especially, perhaps, are pressured into thinking that the approval of God is only to be gained by cleaning up their lives in the same way that you might clean up your house and get your family sorted out. A bit like this.

Once I've cleaned this house up properly,
I honestly think I'll get somewhere.
Once I've pulled out every single piece of furniture and used an
    abrasive cloth with strong stuff on it,
I think I shall come to grips with the rest of my life.
Once I've put everything into separate piles, each containing the
    same sort of thing (if you know what I mean),
I think I'll manage.
Once I've written a list that includes absolutely everything,
I think the whole business will seem very much clearer.
Once I've had time to work slowly from one item to another,
I'm sure things will change.
Once I've eaten sensibly for more than a week and a half,
Once I've sorted out the things that are my fault,
Once I've sorted out the things that are not my fault,
Once I've spent a little more time reading useful books,
Being with people I like,
Getting out into the air,
Making bread,
Drinking less,
Drinking more,
Going to the theatre, adopting a third-world child,
Eating free-range eggs,

And writing long letters,
Once I've pulled every single piece of furniture *right out*,
And cleaned this house up properly,
Once I've become somebody else,
I honestly think I'll get somewhere.

The Unlocking

DEAR FAMILY

My family has brought me much joy, but also the discovery of a new kind of pain, something to do with unavoidable engagement and being forced to observe the gradual death of innocence. It is even more, I think, to do with my own shortcomings as a father and a husband. I must be honest, though, and say that these things always seem very much worse at night.

Dear family, I write to you in this campfire place
Where temporary flames repel the savage things
Whose glowing hungry eyes appear from time to time
They know, as I do, that a campfire only burns as long as fuel lasts
My stocks are low as ever, and these devils never rest
But I have light and time enough to write to you
Dear family, asleep, for once, beside me here in peace
To say how I regret the need to share such fearful travelling with you
I know that monster-ridden darkness is my own affair
I have no right to take you there
The battle I shall face tonight will threaten you
But certainly it never was your fight
God knows I wish that it was otherwise
That we could strike our camp and head for home
I have some choice
But when those creatures leap I find I am clean out of choice
And they draw blood so easily
Dear family, as you awake
And eye my campfire ashes nervously
I want to say how I am wretchedly aware

That others would protect and lead you properly
They would be strong and confident and sure
They would be many things that I will never be
I only know they could not love you more

Cabbages for the King

FEAR OF
NOTHING

Ghosts is a novel about a group of people who were in the same youth group at church but have not met for twenty years. They gather for a weekend in a house that is said to be one of the most haunted houses in England. Each person has agreed that, in the course of the weekend, they will name and talk about the thing that they fear most. For one of the characters, a man named Graham, the most profound fear is linked to failure in relation to his family.

The narrator is David Herrick, recently widowed and only very reluctantly present.

"No," said Graham, "what I was meaning to say was that I'm terrified – yes, I think terrified is the word – of there being nothing after we die. Just lately I've even had trouble sleeping because of it. I lie awake, you see, just thinking about Julie and the girls and all the little things we do and say and feel, and I think to myself – what if it's all rubbish that gets thrown away in the end? What if none of it really means anything? What if there is no God and no heaven and no being together again after we die? And I think, well, if there isn't, I'd almost rather die now and stop all the pretending and the – the silly hoping."

His eyes widened and his voice broke a little as he went on.

"I can't help it. At night, over and over again, I see my little girls' eyes all big and round when they're curled up in their bunks and I'm telling them about Jesus. You know, they look at me with such – such trust and believe all the things that I say. They ask me questions, and I answer them, and they nod. We sing things together and pray. But the trouble is, I'm not sure that *I* believe what I say. I tell them Grandma's safe in heaven and they're going to see her again one day. But what if she isn't?" His voice rose to a little crescendo, filled with the panic that must have been lying just below the surface for a very long time. "What if it's all just a cruel, nasty joke, and at the end of all these things that seemed to mean *so much* there's nothing? There are times when – when I want to go to a lonely place and just sort of scream and howl!" He collected himself with an effort and glanced around apologetically. "I don't, of course."

The first line of a poem passed through my mind. 'I took my daughter to the park last night ...'

"There is a heaven," said Peter simply, after a pause, "and Jesus will be there and so will you and your wife and your little girls and their grandma."

"Oh, yes. Yes!" Graham nodded vigorously, as though Peter had proposed a subtle, telling argument that successfully counteracted his fears. "Yes, of course. Thank you ..."

Unconvincing. If there was one thing I had learned from contact with troubled people over the years, it was that spiritual problems are very often not spiritual problems at all. Losing weight, for instance, could be as effective as anything in restoring a faltering relationship with God. There was something else behind Graham's dread of oblivion.

"Graham, do you mind if I ask you something?"

"No, David, not at all, of course not."

"What is your worst worry about you and your family – your very worst worry?"

Graham blinked, then hunted everywhere with his eyes, searching for an escape route that I suspected he didn't really want to find.

"Angela," he said very quietly at last, "I wonder – do you think I might have a glass of wine, or – or whisky even, *after* I've said what I'm going to say?"

Angela rocked back on her heels and spread her arms expansively. "Graham, the entire contents of the drinks cupboard is at your disposal if you really want it. I made the rule so I can jolly well dump it."

"Thank you, Angela. I err, I don't usually deal with things in that way, you understand."

"No, of course not."

"Right. Good. By the way, the things we say here this weekend, they are – you know – confidential, aren't they?"

We all nodded emphatic agreement. Or anyway, I thought privately, about as confidential as it's possible to get with human beings. When Graham spoke again it was virtually in a whisper.

"Sometimes I long for my family to die."

It was like one of those key moments in a film or a play when one of the characters says something that moves the proceedings in a radically different direction or onto another plane altogether. I hoped no one would feel bound to say anything too quickly in response to this extraordinary statement. They didn't. Graham studied the floor and spread his fingers on the arms of his chair as he went on.

"Sometimes – sometimes I imagine that I'm sitting at home reading a newspaper or listening to Radio 4, and a telephone call comes. When I answer it they tell me that Julie and the girls have all been killed in this bad traffic accident." He glanced up and, lifting one hand from his chair, moved it in a gesture of denial from side to side. "Not – I don't mean one where they're hurt or injured. Nothing like that. They've just died instantly and at exactly the same moment – suddenly, you know, without even knowing that anything's happened. No pain, no crying, no being afraid. Just – gone. The police stated that death was instantaneous – that's what they say, isn't it? And I get really upset and everything, and we have the funeral and all the people come to the house for – the get-together, and then they go, and I'm off work for a while with compassionate leave, and then it all settles down and I go back to work and I don't get married again and everything's all right."

Graham's voice filled with emotion as he continued. He was entreating us to understand, to know what it felt like to be inside him.

"You see, the thing is, if it were to happen round about now, if it stopped here, I wouldn't have done *too* badly, would I? I mean, I've tried very hard and it's been all right. I really have tried. I've tried beyond what I am. It's all not too bad. Julie still loves me. That can't go on for ever. It can't! The girls – my girls think I'm really special and funny and okay. They respect me." He shook his head rapidly from side to side. "But they're only little. One day they won't. I know they won't. How on earth could they? I've managed to hold it together up to now. If it ended today or tomorrow or next week I could be at peace for the rest of my life without ever feeling guilty, because it would just be a thing that happened. I could go to work during the day and sit quietly at home in the evening and – and feel sad and listen to the radio." He raised his eyes and looked straight at me. "Do you think I sound like – like an awful monster, David?"

I smiled and shook my head. "No, Graham, I don't. I'll tell you what you sound like. You sound to me like a very good, very loving man with a very lucky family. You sound like someone who finds it extremely difficult to believe in himself as a husband or as a father. You sound like a man who just can't believe that he's done so well at the things he always thought he'd fail at. You sound like someone who's got his faith wrapped round his fears and needs to do a bit of disentangling. And, as a matter of interest, I happen to know for a fact that you're very far from being alone in thinking the way you do."

"Graham, all that stuff about road accidents," put in Jenny, "if you don't mind me saying so, I think that's just a fantasy, a sort of escape valve to stop you going off pop when you start thinking about the next twenty years instead of keeping your eyes on tonight and tomorrow morning. Fantasies aren't usually about what you really want."

She paused and glanced at me, then back at him.

"Besides, if someone really did give you a choice between your wife and your beloved little girls being there when you get home tomorrow, or discovering that something bad had happened to them while you were away, which would you choose? I mean – look – suppose I really did have the power to make it happen. You choose. You can go home and find that they're all dead and gone, killed in that accident you were talking about, or you can have them running up and throwing their arms round you because you're back. Think about it now. Think about their faces. Choose, Graham. Which do you want?"

There was no need for him to answer. His face said it all. There was a new light in his eyes. It happens very rarely, but just occasionally the opportunity to confess has an almost instantaneous effect. If it had been a halfway reasonable thing to do, I think Graham might have shot straight out of the door, jumped in his car, and driven through the night to get to the people he loved. Good for him,

"Such a – a relief!" he said. "So silly."

•—◆—•

Ghosts

ADRIAN'S REAL
SUPPORT GROUP

The Sacred Diarist has decided that, after the popularity of his writings he needs a "support group", especially now that he is receiving so many invitations to speak in all sorts of church-related venues. Not a bad idea, but do you want people who will flatter you or people who will tell the truth – and which is the most important support group of all?

Tuesday 1 Feb

Decided this morning that I ought to have one of those support groups that lots of other Christian speakers have. The more I pictured it the more I liked it. I would be God's chosen vehicle, powerful and mantled with authority in public, yet restrained and full of grace in private, opening myself up in humble submission to the ministrations, advice, and criticism of a little group of folk who would feel privileged and proud to be part of what God was doing through me.

Mentioned the idea to Anne and Gerald over breakfast.

"The thing is," I said, "that I'd submit myself to their advice and criticism and be sort of accountable to them, and er . . . that sort of thing."

Anne stopped in mid-toast-buttering, did a little laugh, and said, "But you absolutely *hate* criticism, darling. You always have done. You get very cross indeed when anyone says anything remotely critical – doesn't he, Gerald?"

"Mum's right, Dad," said Gerald, "criticism's one of the things that makes little bits of spit appear at the corners of your mouth."

Absolutely appalled by this response to my idea. "I do *not* hate criticism, Anne – I've never heard such rubbish in my life! How can you possibly say that? I have been given the heart of a servant."

Gerald said, "I don't think the transplant's taken, Dad."

Ignored him.

"And I do not get 'very cross'. You make me sound like – like a toddler who's been told he can't have another sweet. I'll have you know that God has done a mighty work of building in me as far as the whole area of criticism's concerned. Frankly, you couldn't be more wrong if you tried."

Both burst into laughter at this point, for reasons that totally escape me. Gerald so busy cackling he didn't realise the end of his hair had flopped into the marmalade. I was slightly consoled by this.

When she'd recovered, Anne said, "I'm sorry, Adrian, I'm sure God has done a mighty work of building in you, it's just that –"

"It hasn't been unveiled yet."

"No, Gerald, don't – that's not what I was going to say. What I was going to say," Anne continued in her sensible voice, "was that you *have* changed. You're quite right. You *are* much more aware of problems and faults in yourself that, in the past, you never even noticed. But let's be honest, darling, you're still not very good at – well, hearing about them from other people, are you? There's something useful and rather splendid about telling big halls full of people that you're not a very good person, but you're completely in charge of what people are allowed to know about you in that sort of situation, aren't you? In fact, they think all the more of you for being so honest about your shortcomings, so, in a sense, you win all ways, don't you? And that's great, as long as you can also take a bit of criticism from people like us, who are close to you and aren't going to be quite so easily impressed."

She reached over and took my hand. "I'm sorry, darling. Gerald and I shouldn't have laughed at you like that just then. It was just so funny that you got very cross indeed when I criticised the fact that you get very cross indeed whenever you're criticised. Well, you did, didn't you? Adrian, you do see what I'm getting at, don't you?"

Paralysed temporarily by the battle raging inside me. Didn't want to appear sulky or angry because both were bound to be interpreted as failure to accept criticism, but didn't want to speak, knowing it would come out sounding sulky or angry because that's how I actually felt. Managed a sort of glassy-eyed, wooden nodding movement.

"If it's any use to you, Dad," said Gerald, who'd been scribbling on the back of an envelope, "here's a little verse on the subject:

"Freely I confess my sins,
For God has poured his Grace in,
But when another lists my faults,
I want to smash his face in.

"Does that more or less sum it up?"

Couldn't help laughing. Anne made more coffee.

I said, "So you don't think the support group idea is a good one?"

"Oh, yes," said Anne, "I think it's an excellent idea, as long as you're going to be genuinely vulnerable and not just use it as a means of – well, emphasising and relishing your 'stardom'. That's not what you want, is it?"

Made me sound like Liberace.

"Oh, no . . . no, that would be awful. I'd hate that . . ."

"You don't want to waste their time either, do you? Tell you what – why don't you ask Edwin to choose a group and set the whole thing up for you? He'll know the best people to ask."

"Oh," I said, "I was rather thinking that I might choose who comes."

"Exactly," said Anne and Gerald in chorus.

Reluctantly but sincerely thanked God for my family before going to bed tonight.

• ◆ •

Sacred Diary of Adrian Plass, Christian Speaker,
Aged Forty-Five and Three Quarters

CHILDREN OF
THE NIGHT

I meet so many people who feel that they have failed their children in matters of faith and church attendance. I am one of them myself. All those tears and prayers, and they seem as far from God as ever. But I am beginning to believe that God will faithfully answer those prayers at the right time, and I also believe that some of our children come to him by night.

> Now there was a man of the Pharisees named Nicodemus, a member of the Jewish ruling council. He came to Jesus at night and said, "Rabbi, we know you are a teacher who has come from God. For no one could perform the miraculous signs you are doing if God were not with him."
>
> In reply Jesus declared, "I tell you the truth, no one can see the kingdom of God unless he is born again."
>
> "How can a man be born when he is old?" Nicodemus asked. "Surely he cannot enter a second time into his mother's womb to be born!"
>
> Jesus answered, "I tell you the truth, no one can enter the kingdom of God unless he is born of water and the Spirit."
>
> John 3 : 1–5

I suspect that, throughout history, a surprisingly large section of the Christian Church has only visited Jesus by night. In the heartsick early hours, or at times when the world has receded like a tide, they tiptoe warily into his presence bringing with them the same burning acknowledgement of who he is, and the same searching questions, as Nicodemus brought two thousand years ago.

This army of secret admirers has probably included every class, race, and type of person that ever existed, but I would like, just for a moment, to think about the young people of this age and the difficulties they face in publicly relating to Jesus.

We adults don't help. I know that there have been times when I would have cheerfully exchanged all ideals of reality and integrity for the comfortable knowledge that my children were uncomplicated, incurious, card-carrying members of a chorus-singing, sausage-sizzling, sex-avoiding, Bible-studying, evangelical church youth-group. There's nothing wrong with all those things, of course. Some of them are very right. But my concern was not actually for their relationship with Jesus. I just wanted them out of harm's way so that I could find peace of mind.

You can't always have your parental cake and eat it. Many parents bring their children up to believe that it's all right to question and test and be who they are. They may not have had some kind of grand organised plan, and they may have made horrendous mistakes from time to time, but they do want them to have those qualities and that freedom. Their children might not, therefore, be the kind of kids who will ever be safely slotted into the sort of formal situation that I described (caricatured) just now. Many unchurched children will certainly have encountered God in the course of their lives, and their parents may be asking his blessing on them constantly, but perhaps, for the time being at least, they will be visiting Jesus by night, and he has to be trusted to deal with them. I think many of us would be astonished to learn how much is happening in the hearts and minds of the non-attending young people who cause us so much concern.

I would hate anyone to think that I was expressing anti-church views. I belong to one myself, and I support everything that it does. Some youth groups are truly excellent and relevant. But my heart aches for the vast numbers of young people from both Christian and non-Christian families, who simply cannot fit into such a situation and go on being who they are.

Christianity is not defined by the morning or the evening services, however good and necessary they might be.

Christianity is not defined by a way of speaking or dressing or doing religious things or aiming for vaguely middle-class norms.

Christianity is not defined by membership of the school Christian Union, however genuine, hard-working, and prayerful.

Christianity is not defined by witnessing to class-mates, however admirable and right that may sometimes be.

Christianity is not about teenagers making their parents feel safe by conforming to a particular sub-culture.

Christianity is about an encounter with God. It's about the need to turn from the negative past. It's about the need to be embraced by the warm and excited forgiveness of the Father. It's about discovering that it is possible to start again – to be born again. It's about understanding just a little of the sacrifice that Jesus made in dying on the cross. It's about establishing a lasting friendship with that same risen Jesus.

We can teach a young person some of these things, but the real negotiations have to be carried out privately between him or herself and the Master, and sometimes that has to happen secretly, in the night.

Meanwhile, those of us who are worried will go on praying, and do our best to trust him.

Pray with Me

We cry out to you for our young people, Father – not that they should conform to cultural or institutional expectations, but that they should meet you, Lord. That's what we want. Whether they come by conventional or eccentric routes is of no consequence. What matters is that they come to you with the needs and questions and problems that only you can deal with. Some of our churches are truly representing you, but many have become museums of tedium. We adults have allowed that to happen, and we ask your forgiveness. We want to change things for the better. In the meantime, protect and watch over those who have drifted away, Father. When they come to you by night, may they learn how much you love them. Amen.

•—◆—•

The Unlocking

MARK AND
CHURCH

Speaking of which, Mark from the *Stress Family Robinsons* has never enjoyed church. In fact he hates it, and now the whole thing has come to a head. Dip tells the story.

"I don't mind God, but church is crap."

I almost choked on my vanilla slice. I don't know why I found it quite so funny, except that as soon as Mark had spoken I formed a mental picture of Almighty God seated majestically upon his throne, receiving that harassed angel whose job it is to monitor the progress of the Robinsons. "What news of the boy Mark?" the creator of the universe would enquire impressively, and, as the mighty hosts of heaven leaned forward in solemn expectation, the angel would reply, "He says he doesn't mind God but church is crap."

Perhaps my view of God's nature is a mistaken one, but I suspect that far from dipping automatically into the thunderbolt box, he might have smiled a little to himself on hearing this and said, "Well first of all, it is, of course, immensely flattering to hear that Mark doesn't mind me, and as for the second point, well, I wouldn't have put it quite like that myself, but the lad does have a point."

Fortunately I managed to prevent the involuntary distribution of my vanilla slice and to keep a straight face, because neither Kathy nor Mike had found anything amusing about Mark's comment. Kathy, presumably not trusting herself to speak, turned to Mike with a "Get the Thunderbolts out" expression on her face but Mark had not finished.

"Church is boring and goes on forever and I hate it. If I was God I wouldn't go. Mum *please* let me stop going. I can't stand it any longer. I feel all big and red and ugly when I'm sittin' there. Don't make me go any more – I'll do the dinner washing-up every Sunday instead."

This implicit equating of church attendance with household chores brought a smile to Mike's face, but all of Kathy's spirit was gone. She seemed to have sagged into complete defeat. She barely had the energy to speak.

"I hope you know, Mark, that God is very important to me. I think Jesus died for me so that God could be my father, and I've been trying to understand what that means ever since I – well, since I became part of it. I mess things up in all sorts of ways, but right deep down inside I think I know I love God, and he loves me – although I lose my way a bit with that sometimes. So, what I'm saying is that, however it might seem, even if the church blew up tomorrow morning and I couldn't go any more, there'd still be God and Jesus and me. It isn't just how it looks to other people – although I'm afraid that seems to really matter to me sometimes – it's about me hoping you'll know God as well one day. That's the only thing that matters in the end." She looked at Mike. "I think we ought to let Mark stop going to church for the moment, except for Christmas and things – only if you agree, of course, Mike."

Mike nodded judicially. "I'm happy to go along with that as long as Mark is quite clear that this is a decision made by us, and that we shall expect there to be no arguments on those occasions when we do require him to attend church with us."

Despite being addressed by his father as if he was an applicant at some land tribunal, there was no doubt that Mark understood what was being said. It was lovely to watch. He sat bolt upright in his chair and stared open-mouthed at his mother, hardly able to take in the fact that his weekly torture was over.

"So I don't have to go tomorrow?"

"You don't have to go tomorrow," she confirmed in the same weak voice she had used before.

Mark, driven to an excessive show of emotion by sheer relief and excitement, crossed the room at a most un-Mark like speed and threw his arms round his mother's neck. "Oh, thanks, Mum!" Those were, I think, the words that emerged in a rather muffled state from this unexpected embrace. The miraculous effect on Kathy, though predictable to anyone who knew her, still amazed me. It was as if she had been instantaneously and totally healed, like one of those New Testament sufferers who encountered Jesus. One sudden, substantial dose of physical and verbal affection, when she thought the medicine bottle might be empty, and her whole being was transformed. When she spoke her voice had regained its vibrancy.

"You might as well go and spread the good news to your friends."

"All right." Mark, grabbing the shining moment, headed for the door, pausing only to say, "Thanks, Mum – thanks, Dad." Just before disappearing he flashed one of his film-star smiles at me – a real sizzler it was. After that we heard hurried coat-flapping noises as he got ready to go out in the rain, and then there was a short silence during which I believe that, in the solitude of the hall, Mark raised his eyes, bent his arm, and shook a triumphant fist towards the ceiling, this being the gesture that traditionally accompanies the universal victory cry of the fourteen-year-old.

"Yes-s-s!" we heard him cry exultantly. "Yes-s-s!"

• ◆ •

Stress Family Robinson

HELPING WITH
THE MESS

It's terribly hard to grasp that the love of God is often more accessible when we are in a mess than at those times when we feel we've got everything under control. Here we join *Never Mind the Reversing Ducks,* a book that offers companionship and comment to readers of the gospel according to Saint Mark. Read on ...

Jesus went out again beside the sea; the whole crowd gathered around him, and he taught them. As he was walking along, he saw Levi son of Alphaeus sitting at the tax booth, and he said to him, "Follow me." And he got up and followed him.

And as he sat at dinner in Levi's house, many tax collectors and sinners were also sitting with Jesus and his disciples—for there were many who followed him.

When the scribes of the Pharisees saw that he was eating with sinners and tax collectors, they said to his disciples, "Why does he eat with tax collectors and sinners?"

When Jesus heard this, he said to them, "Those who are well have no need of a physician, but those who are sick; I have come to call not the righteous but sinners."

Mark 2 : 13 – 17 NRSV

Pretty good ploy this on Jesus' part, don't you think? I don't know if Zaccheus or Levi came first, but the pattern seems to be the same. Save a tax collector and you get asked to dinner. Only joking. I'm sure it never crossed his mind. Well – almost sure.

Jesus' desire and willingness to move right into the homes and hearts of the sad, the bad, and the greedy was and is a jewel in the crown of his ministry. The Pharisees were quite unable to accept it, and I imagine one or two of the sinners had a bit of a problem taking it in. They still do. I still do sometimes.

I remember, for instance, a particular fortnight around the end of August and beginning of September in the first year of this century.

The year had begun with the sad death of our dear dog, Rosie, who had grown up with our children, but, being in the midst of hectic preparations for the blessing of my oldest son's marriage, we barely had a moment to mourn her passing. Matthew had married his charming Azeri bride, Alina, briefly and technically in Turkey earlier that year. Now they were anxious to do the thing properly, and they wanted "the works". They wanted to be married by a proper vicar in a proper country church, wearing proper wedding clothes with proper guests and a proper wedding reception afterwards. And, of course, ideally it would happen on a proper sunny English day in early September.

Their wishes were granted. That year the second of September was one of those perfect days when nothing goes wrong and the laughter and tears and other weather all happen in just the right places. It couldn't have been more – proper.

A thrilling facet of this sparkling jewel of an occasion was the presence of Alina's parents, Irina and Oleg, who flew all the way from Baku, the capital of Azerbaijan, on the evening before the wedding, to be with their daughter on her special day. Azerbaijan is a bureaucratic nightmare. Arranging visas and tickets had been a long, exhausting business for us all. But now, excitingly, if improbably, these two non-English-speaking inhabitants of an oil-producing ex-Soviet republic were comfortably ensconced in a farmhouse bed-and-breakfast establishment just down the road. Unbelievable.

It was in the week after the wedding that my neurosis began to set in. Our house had been occupied and eaten in every day by at least ten people, sometimes twelve. This was fine except that I am famous – or rather infamous – for my dislike of clutter and untidiness. Members of my family alternate between derision and annoyance in their response to this aspect of my personality, but there's nothing I can do about it, I'm afraid. I am capable of a sort of cataclysmic untidiness of my own on rare occasions, but the point is that I select those occasions, if you see what I mean.

During that second week I began to understand how servants working in large houses in the Victorian and Edwardian eras must have felt during every day of their lives. Hoovering and washing-up and laying tables and putting things away and preparing meals and taking rubbish to the council tip and shopping and sorting everything out was exhausting. Not, I hasten to add, in case my wife reads this, that I laboured alone. We all worked hard. No, it was just that this completion neurosis of mine drove me past the point of reasonable endeavour, producing a state of wild-eyed frustration in me whenever some innocent soul committed the unforgivable sin of moving a coffee table five degrees away from an exact right-angle, or placed a coffee-cup on a polished surface without using a coaster. Sad, isn't it?

For the first few days of this feverish activity, though I say it myself, I handled things pretty well. I quite enjoyed an inner, heroic posturing in the role of one working selflessly for the sake of others. I was the host who not only welcomed and entertained, but also laboured ceaselessly behind the scenes with no thought of reward or gratitude. How impressed they must be, I reflected, by the way the house is magically sorted out in their absence each day, calm and ordered in readiness for their return. A good witness too, I thought smugly (may God forgive me!), for Christians to offer those from a distant, pagan land.

At around lunchtime on the thirteenth day I simply ran out of steam and goodwill. Why the dickens was I bothering to clean up after people who just came in and messed it all up again? What was the point? When were they going to acknowledge the hard work I'd been doing? They probably hadn't even noticed. Huh! Fancy coming all this way from a foreign country and letting me slave away like a – like a slave. I felt tired and irritable and fed-up . . .

That morning I sat at my desk, head in hands, surveying the wreckage of my good intentions and the disintegration of my so-called Christian witness. The dwelling place of my faith was in a state of complete disarray, quite unsuitable for visitors. It was at that moment that the gentle voice of Jesus said, very quietly, "May I come in?"

"Well," I replied, almost tearfully, "it's a bit of a mess, actually."

"Oh, I've never minded that," he said, "I'll give you a hand clearing up."

"Thank you," I said, and I meant it.

He calls on the strangest people at the strangest times, doesn't he? Ready?

• ◆ •

Never Mind the Reversing Ducks

Part Two

COMMUNICATION

I have included a whole section on communication because it is, or ought to be, such a
crucial factor in successful family life – whatever
that is. When we prevent people close to us
from having access to any part of our inner lives
there's likely to be trouble. Talk and listen.
Those seem to be the two essentials.
Let's do a little exploring in this area.

FELICITY AND
THE THESAURUS

Up to a certain age, children are usually very good at making real contact with others – indeed, they take a pleasure in it. Here's Felicity Robinson in the second *Stress Family Robinson* book. This time the narrator is Kathy.

"Mummy, I've got a question for you. Which is the most frightening prehistoric monster of all, more frightening than Tyrannosaurus Rex or raptors or any of those on the film you wouldn't let me see, and Daddy did? Jack just wrote it down for me."

Felicity was indeed once more among us, bright with her interest in whatever it was she wanted to communicate. Jack was her oldest brother, just back from his final term at university and working through one of the local job agencies during the week while he considered the little matter of what to do with the rest of his life. Jack never seemed to get out of his bed unless there was some exceptionally good reason for doing so. Today was Saturday and there was not even a bad reason for surfacing. No doubt his little sister had jumped on him, ignored his groans, and demanded entertainment. Their relationship was a constant joy to me. I had been so afraid that when Jack went away Felicity would lose touch with the feeling of closeness there had been between them for the first few years of her life. Not a sign of it.

"Go on, then," I said, "let's hear it."

"Okay." She cleared her throat and read from her piece of paper. "The most frightening dinosaur of all is one that has not become extinct like all the other dinosaurs but can still be found in this present age, lurking in libraries, studies, and bookshops all over England. It is called the Thesaurus, and it is huge, massive, very large, enormous, gar – gargantuan, colossal, king-size, monstrous, immense, titanic, and vast. Because of this, anyone who sees, observes, spots, notices, views, perceives, regards, witnesses, or looks at it, is likely to be terrified, aghast, petrified, scared, shocked, alarmed, and windy. *Windy!*" she repeated with a peal of laughter, "I think I'd be windy if I saw a dinosaur. Maybe that would put it off eating me."

"Well, it would me. Just as a matter of interest, darling daughter," I said, "do you know what a thesaurus really is?"

"Yes, Mummy," she replied calmly, referring once more to her sheet of paper, "it is a collection of concepts or words arranged according to sense. What did you think it was?" She grinned. "Jack said you'd ask me that."

◆–◆–◆

Stress Family Robinson – The Birthday Party

THE LOVE OF TRUTH
OR THE TRUTH OF LOVE

Communicating important truths to our children can be a very challenging business. This account of a conversation with our son Matthew when he was about twelve years old is a prime example. It comes from *Cabbages for the King*, a collection of sketches, poems, and stories published in the early nineties.

A few years ago we enjoyed a family holiday in Denmark, and I can testify that there's a lot more to that ancient kingdom than bacon and Lego. The eastern peninsula that we explored was beautiful to look at and full of interest. More importantly from the point of view of our three boys, there was a football pitch and two practise goals just up the road from our holiday house in the village of Stenvad. It was a comfortable place to stay, with a "cricket sized" garden at the back.

We had some very silly jokes from some members of the family. The worst was the suggestion that when we got home we should take our films into the chemist, then when we returned to collect them a few days later we would say:

"May we have Hamlet please?"

"Hamlet?" the shop assistant would enquire.

"Yes," we would reply, "the prints of Denmark."

Gettit?

The best thing as usual was just being together as a family, arguing in peace for once.

Sometimes the holiday ethos allows quite subtle problems to rise to the surface.

One evening, after the younger members of the family had finally been coaxed, threatened, and bribed to bed, my oldest son put into words an area of concern that had never occurred to me. He described how, as he listened to Bridget and me talking to the younger children, praising them for things they'd said or bought or done, he recognised in the words we used and the tone of our voices, the same kind of encouragement that had enabled him to feel valued and approved of as he grew up. Now, however, seeing how positive we were about quite small efforts and achievements on the part of the little ones, he started to feel a little insecure. Perhaps we had been less than sincere when we praised him in the past. What if his feelings of alrightness were based on a series of half truths? Maybe we weren't really proud of him after all.

I didn't really know what to say in reply to this, but by the next morning the issue had resolved itself into a question in my mind: Which is more important in relationships, the love of truth or the truth of love? Should our response to the efforts of others be doggedly, uncompromisingly accurate, or should we let love mould and modify our reactions.

I tried to explain what I was thinking to my son, but it was only when I got down to concrete examples in his own life that he began to see what I meant.

"What about you with Katy?" I said (Katy was three and her biggest brother was potty about her). "What about when Katy brings you one of her drawings and asks what you think of it? Do you say, 'I'm sorry Kate, but its just a meaningless scribble?' or do you say, 'Well done Katy, that's really lovely!' In fact," I went on, seeing his face soften, "would you be happy if you knew that the way I feel about you is the same as the way you feel about Katy?"

"Yes," he said, "I would."

"That's good, then," I said, "because it is."

The maintenance and repair of relationships with God, family, neighbours, and fellow believers is an absolute priority in our lives, but what a tricky area this can be.

• ◆ •

Cabbages for the King

CISSY'S
PRAYER

Children's attempts to communicate with God can be moving and some-times very funny. This little girl (who appears in *A Year at St Yorick's*) seems to be somewhat confused in her theology.

God i want to pray that my favrit lamb binky from our farm will go to hevven and be with us all after we die I think he will cos I have eaten him so he is inside me like jesus some bits of him are inside a sorted uther members of our fammily but pleese will you put him back together when you get all the bits in it will be a bit of a jig saw puzzel but i know you can do it dont bother with the one called frank cos he allways butted me with his head amen

A Year at St Yorick's

THE REAL
PROBLEM

Sometimes our behaviour can communicate a truth that we would not care to face or own. Even when we do face it, we are not always willing to allow others to be involved. As the last line of the poem indicates, there is a need for communication of some of our problems to the family of the church if we really want to solve them. It is fear of vulnerability and condemnation that prevents us from being open. As a body, we could be so much more mutually valuable if we trusted each other.

This is the first extract from a book called *Clearing Away the Rubbish*, another collection of sketches, poems, and songs, written and published in the late eighties.

I was a rather troubled little boy. Things confused me. I remember feeling particularly anxious about the difference between the way my father was in church every Sunday and his behaviour at home before and after the service. The hour that we spent in the little Roman Catholic chapel at the end of the village was, all too frequently, sandwiched between much longer periods of anger and tumult. I found it difficult to understand how Dad could switch so easily into a smiling civilized mode, purely, it seemed to me, for the benefit of church acquaintances who never had to witness the scenes of domestic tension and conflict that sprang so easily from his profound insecurity. I wondered why God didn't sort it out. I knew I would have done if I'd been omnipotent.

Nowadays, with three sons under fourteen and a baby daughter who's nearly a year old, it still requires something akin to a small civil war to get everyone clean and dressed and actually moving towards the family service in our local Anglican church. Threats are hissed, small indignant faces are washed, coats are unearthed, the dog, who has tried to follow us, is taken back and incarcerated, and we are on our way at last, usually in a less than holy frame of mind. The difference between my children's experience of Sunday mornings and my own early memories is, I hope, that as a family we are much more honest with ourselves and outsiders than my father ever felt able to be. Thank God for that. Some still aren't able to be that honest.

The Real Problem is a simple little poem, expressing this particular problem from the child's point of view. Bridget and I usually adopt child-like tones when performing it, but it isn't really essential. The point is in the words. It is usually received with a low hum of identification ...

Sunday is a funny day,
It starts with lots of noise.
Mummy rushes round with socks,
And Daddy shouts, "You boys!"

Then Mummy says, "Now don't blame them,
You know you're just as bad,
You've only just got out of bed,
It really makes me mad!"

My mummy is a Christian,
My daddy is as well,
My mummy says, "Oh, heavens!"
My daddy says, "Oh, hell!"

And when we get to church at last,
It's really very strange,
'Cos Mum and Dad stop arguing,
And suddenly they change.

At church my mum and dad are friends,
They get on very well,
But no one knows they've had a row,
And I'm not gonna tell.

People often come to them,
Because they seem so nice,
And Mum and Dad are very pleased
To give them some advice.

They tell them Christian freedom
Is worth an awful lot,
But I don't know what freedom means,
If freedom's what they've got.

Daddy loves the meetings,
He's always at them all,
He's learning how to understand
The letters of St Paul.

But Mummy says, "I'm stuck at home
To lead my Christian life,
It's just as well for blinkin' Paul
He didn't have a wife."

I once heard my mummy say
She'd walk out of his life,
I once heard Daddy say to her
He'd picked a rotten wife.

They really love each other,
I really think they do.
I think the people in the church
Would help them – if they knew.

Clearing Away the Rubbish

ADRIAN'S
CHILDREN'S TALK

Communicating with your own children can be bad enough, let alone trying to get through to other people's. Here we are, back in *Sacred Diary* world, and Adrian has foolishly allowed himself to be flattered into giving the children's talk at a local church. The vicar introduces him.

"Now may I say, on behalf of all of us, and especially the little ones, how pleased we are to welcome Mr Adrian Plass, who will be doing our children's talk this morning. Mr Plass has written some gloriously funny books and is well known as a very fine speaker, so we all look forward with immense pleasure to hearing what he has to say to us. Thank you."

Nearly paralysed with nerves by the time I stood up to talk to the children. Felt as if I was trying to swallow a large apple whole, smile, and speak simultaneously. Decided the only hope of keeping their attention was to make an impact right at the beginning.

I said, "Right, who'd like to hear a *really* scary story?"

So far, so good. All the children and a selection of indulgently smiling, roguishly uninhibited, crinkly-eyed adults put their hands up.

"The only thing is – I'm not sure if I ought to tell you this story, because it's very, very, *very* frightening. In fact it's *so* frightening that I might make myself scream with fear just by telling it to you. In fact, it's probably the most terrifying story *anyone, anywhere* has *ever* heard in the whole history of telling stories."

Certainly seemed to have succeeded in making an impact on everybody. Noticed that the indulgent smiles on the faces of most of the crinkly-eyed adults had faded. A small, round-faced, rosy-cheeked, pigtailed girl of about three glanced worriedly over her shoulder to check Mummy and Daddy were still in the church.

I said, in low, menacing tones, "Ready to be sick with fear, then?"

Might have overdone it a bit. The children were a solid block of tension and dread, holding on to each other for safety and staring at me, wide-eyed with apprehension. Certainly paying attention.

Ruined the whole effect right at the beginning with a stupid, unintentional spoonerism.

I said, "Once upon a time, there was a crappy little gab called Hordon . . ."

Short, shocked, uncomprehending silence. An elderly lady at the back of the church cupped her hand behind her ear and said, "Once upon a time there was a *what*, did he say . . . ?"

The small pigtailed girl turned round and said in a loud, clear voice, "He said there was a crappy little gab called Hordon, but I don't know what crappy means, and I don't know what a gab is, and I've never heard of anyone called 'Hordon'. What is a crappy little gab called Hordon? What does *crappy* mean? Is it –"

Panicked and interrupted hurriedly. "I didn't say the story was about a crappy little gab called Hordon." Expressions of outraged disbelief appeared on the faces of the children. "Or rather – sorry, sorry – I did say that, but it was a mistake. What I meant to say was that once upon a time there was a happy little crab called Gordon. And one day Gordon's big brothers and sisters forgot what their mummy and daddy had told them about looking after Gordon, and while they were doing something else, he wandered off into a different rock pool and was very frightened because a seagull nearly ate him up and his mummy rescued him just in time."

Short silence.

The little girl said, "What happened next?"

"Er, well, that's it – that's the end."

Filled with despair as I realised that I'd left out all the funny crab voices and the conversation between the brothers and sisters and the frightening bit leading up to Gordon's mummy finding him. I'd managed to finish the story in thirty seconds flat.

"That's not what I'd call a very, very *scary* story," said the pigtailed girl. "That's what I'd call a very, very *short* story."

Tried to carry brightly on.

"Right, now who'd like to suggest what the story teaches us?"

Lots of arms went up. Pointed at a thin little girl with huge glasses. She said, "The seaside is a very bad, nasty, dangerous place for small children?"

Two toddlers opened their eyes very wide at this suggestion and, to my horror, seemed to be on the verge of tears.

"No," I said hurriedly, "of course it doesn't mean that. The seaside is a *lovely* place for children. Of course it is."

The two toddlers cheered up immediately. The thin little girl's face crumpled.

"But er . . . it was a very good suggestion – very good indeed. Well done!" Could hear my own voice rising to a hysterical pitch. "Come on, somebody else – what does the story show us?"

A little lad with wide staring eyes and hair standing up on end, who looked as if a powerful electric current was being passed through his body, called out, "Does it show that we must never trust our brothers and sisters, because they just don't care when we get eaten at the seaside?"

Felt as if I was going mad. I know I'd started it, but the whole thing was turning into something out of Edgar Allan Poe. Children's talks aren't supposed to leave the congregation emotionally scarred for life.

"Of course our brothers and sisters care when we get eaten at the seaside. I mean" – hastily – "we're not going to be eaten at the seaside – or anywhere else for that matter, but if we were – *if* we were, then our brothers and sisters would certainly care, of *course* they would. Look, doesn't anyone think," I pleaded desperately, "that the story might show how important it is for us to look after each other? Do you think that's what it shows?"

At this, a pretty little dark-haired thing pushed her hand into the air as far as it would go, waving wildly, rocking her whole body and clenching her teeth with the sheer eagerness of her desire to reply. I nodded encouragingly.

"Do you think that's what it shows?"

She said, "No."

Could feel my whole being moving rapidly into Basil Fawlty mode.

"All right – all right! Everybody put their hands down, and I'll go over it again, okay? No, I said put your hands *down*, didn't I? You all had your chance to say what the story meant just now, and no one's got it right. Now it's my turn, unless of course someone wants to object."

Glared challengingly at the children. They huddled fearfully together for mutual protection and said nothing.

"Now! There's a crab called Gordon. Right?"

Anxious nods.

"He's happy. *Right?*"

More nods.

"His brothers and sisters are supposed to be looking after him. Right? Anybody find that difficult to understand?"

Solemn head shakes.

"But they forget to look after him, and he nearly gets eaten by a seagull. *Right?*"

Slightly more confident nods.

"But Gordon's mother rescues him. *Right?*"

Smiles and nods.

"Good! Excellent! So – what does the story teach us?"

Uneasy pause. Children all looked at each other. At last, a slightly odd, serious-looking, short-haired boy of about ten, dressed in a dark suit and tie, raised his hand.

"Yes?"

"It shows that Satan will sometimes appear to us as a seagull."

Depressed silence.

Gave up, and said, "Amen".

Afterwards, Reverend Spool reacted as if I'd converted the whole of Great Britain.

"*Wonderful!*" he enthused, clasping my hand again, "I'm sure our children were greatly challenged by your message. So much more likely that a lesson will lodge in tiny minds when it comes wrapped up in a well-told story."

Frowns of annoyance directed at me from some of the parents who were trying to soothe their disturbed small children suggested that, given half a chance, they'd like to have lodged something in my tiny mind – a hatchet, for instance. Detached myself as soon as possible from the vicar, who said, just as we were going through the door, "By the way, I have instructed Mr Frobisher that he is to ambush you – yes, positively to *ambush* you – before you leave the church premises. He will be thrilled to defray your expenses. Thank you so much for inspiring us. You must come and speak to the kiddies again soon ..."

Asked Gerald what he'd thought of my talk as we passed through the church porch.

He said, "May I phrase my answer in the form of a cryptic cross-word clue?"

Sighed. "If you must."

"Well, I think it would be something like this."

Handed me another of his infernal backs-of-envelope-jottings. I read it. It said:

RUBBISH FROM CANADA AND FAST MOVING RHYTHMIC VERSE PERFORMED TO MUSICAL BACKING (4 LETTERS)

Gerald said, "And the solution is – "
I said, "I've solved it, thank you very much, and I agree."

❖ ⬥ ❖

The Sacred Diary of Adrian Plass, Christian Speaker,
Aged Forty-Five and Three Quarters

CABLE CAR

There are few people more dangerous than those who think they can speak a foreign language but are in fact deluded. I fear that I am such a person, as you will see. The following passage comes from *View From a Bouncy Castle*, a collection of bite-size anecdotes, stories, and comments about everything under the sun. Here we look at "tact" and what that rare quality actually means.

At one stage in my college education the nature and function of "tact" was explored.

"A tactful person," our lecturer told us, "is one who restores or repairs roles that have become inappropriate, caused embarrassment, or upset relationships."

I got into trouble once, both causing embarrassment and upsetting relationships, during a family holiday in Europe. We were in a cable car on the way up to the top of Mont Blanc. The car was full of tourists, mainly French-speaking, with a smattering of Japanese tourists who uttered very satisfactorily oriental gasps of awe and wonder as the panorama of snow-covered ranges came into view.

A benign, rather stout French lady of advanced years offered my two young sons a sweet each. They, of course, accepted, and it seemed to me an ideal opportunity to demonstrate my profound knowledge of the Gallic tongue.

My wife, sensing from my knitted brows and glazed eyes that I was composing a sentence in French, made frantic attempts to reach me in time to avert disaster, but she was on the other side of the car and didn't make it in time. Tapping the generous lady on the shoulder I smiled warmly and said something that was supposed to mean, "You are obviously a grandmother yourself."

The smile disappeared from the old lady's face as though I had slapped her. Grunts and clicks of disapproval emanated from the other French-speakers. I noticed that my wife gazed intently through the window at nothing at all.

"What did I say?" I hissed. "Was the grammar wrong or something?"

"Unfortunately," said Bridget from the side of her mouth, "you sounded quite confident and fluent. That's what made it so awful!"

"Yes, but what did I say?"

It appeared that what I had said to the lady with the sweets was: "Well you *are* a large woman, aren't you?"

Acute embarrassment and total breakdown in communication.

"The tactful person," my erstwhile lecturer might have said, "would have stepped in with, 'I am sure he was trying to say something complimentary. . . . He didn't mean to upset you. . . .'"

The Christian faith is concerned with breakdown in the relationship between God and man. God created men and women to be in a loving relationship with him, and as long as individuals are not fulfilling this most appropriate of roles there will continue to be a sort of cosmic embarrassment.

I don't know if Jesus' death and resurrection can really be described as the ultimate exercise in tact, but it is the only way I know of repairing the damage that occurred somehow, way back in the past, when, as the Bible has it, Adam and Eve, having spoiled their relationship with God, suddenly recognised their own nakedness and were deeply embarrassed.

● ◆ ●

View From a Bouncy Castle

SWEET NOTHINGS

Contact between husbands and wives should surely be characterised by sweetness and light. Is that the case? Well...

You have stolen my heart, my sister, my bride ... your lips drop sweetness as the honeycomb, my bride; milk and honey are under your tongue. The fragrance of your garments is like that of Lebanon.

Song of Songs 4 : 9–11

I wish I was a little better at the old sweet nothings. Mind you my wife would be deeply suspicious if I suddenly nestled up and told her that honey and milk are under her tongue and the scent of her garments is like the scent of Lebanon. As for claiming that I regard her love as much better than wine – I'm not at all sure she'd believe me.

Seriously, it does seem a pity that many marriages deteriorate not just into a lack of romance, but actual conflict. A dismally common view of marriage is exemplified by a scene I once witnessed in a launderette. As I entered, a loud argument was going on between a man and woman in their early sixties.

"You don't understand listenin' do you?" shouted the lady. "All you can do is make a noise!"

"Go on, get out of it!" returned the man furiously. "You're nothin' but a stupid, mouthy old ratbag!"

"Don't worry!" she snapped, "I don't want to be anywhere you might be!"

And with that, she swept through the door and disappeared.

A pear-shaped lady who had observed these hostilities from beside the drying machines shifted slightly on her seat and addressed the man in dispassionate tones.

"She your wife, then?"

The man stopped muttering and stared at her.

"Married to 'er!" he said incredulously, "I wouldn't marry 'er if she was the last woman on earth!"

"Oh," said the pear-shaped lady, dispassionate as ever, "I thought she must be your wife the way you was talkin' to 'er."

An extreme example of how marriage is seen, perhaps, but it does seem such a shame that so many marriages begin as romances only to decline to the point where your marriage partner is the only person you're ever really nasty to.

When You Walk

MARRIAGE AND AGA COOKERS

Here are the good old Robinsons again, and Kathy is explaining to Dip how conversation at a recent dinner party made her realise that a new effort was needed in communicating her real needs to Mike.

"So what started all this off, then, Kathy?"

"Well . . ."

"Was it suddenly realising fifty is coming towards you like an express train and getting into a bit of a panic because evil, moustachio-twirling life has tied you to the tracks. That's more or less how it felt to me."

"Yes, I think it's been – did you just make up that 'mustachio-twirling life' bit, Dip, or did you have it all prepared? I bet you've been waiting ages for an opportunity to casually trot that out, haven't you?"

She threw her head back and laughed.

"I'm sorry. Is my conversation usually so boring that a sudden pathetic burst of metaphor calls for special celebration? If so, I'll have a small sherry."

"I thought you'd never ask. As you know, we have a small bottle specially set aside for celebration of metaphor, in the grammatical section of the drinks cabinet."

Two minutes later we both had a glass of Bristol Cream in our hands. I took a lovingly reverent sip and decided to answer Dip's question truthfully.

"Mike and I were invited out to dinner a few weeks ago by the Handleys who live in one of those really huge Victorian houses in Swan Road, the ones with the long drives and lovely big sash windows that still work. You know the Handleys, don't you? I think she works up at the charity shop in the precinct most mornings, and Frank was something terribly important to do with the House of Commons before he retired, but not a member of Parliament or anything. They used to go to our church if you remember, then they retired and stopped coming for some reason, and Mike ran into Frank on a committee a couple of months ago and – "

Dip raised a hand in surrender.

"I know who you mean. I never knew them very well, but I *do* know who you mean."

"Well, it doesn't really matter, actually. We never knew them very well either, that was the trouble. So we were both a bit stiff and nervous. Their *house*!" I lowered my voice as though the Handleys might be crouching behind the sofa listening to us. "Dip, I've never seen anything like it. Huge place, all leather and polished wood and antiques and things made out of elephants' feet, and a lady who comes to 'do' for them, you know the sort of thing I mean. I think Mike's just the tiniest bit susceptible to your genuine poshness – "

"Oh, me too, I'm afraid," sighed Dip.

"And he goes into this funny sort of falsely relaxed mode, specially after a couple of drinks – it's difficult to describe, somewhere between sentimentalism and spurious worldly wisdom. Drives me mad because he usually calls on me to support his attempted witticisms or tiny little scraps of homespun philosophy and all I want to do is tell him to shut up."

"But you don't?"

"No, of course I don't, not if I can help it, but with the Handleys I came very close to it. After dinner we got on to the subject of 'marriage in this day and age', and you know how it is at dinner parties with people you don't know very well. Somehow you get carried away on a wave of enthusiastic agreement about absolutely everything in the universe because it's too much like hard work if you don't, and after a while you hear yourself talking absolute piffle or saying things you don't actually go along with at all and your brain goes all numb and dead and you just want to go home and die of shame.

"Anyway, we'd all solemnly agreed that young couples nowadays don't have the moral fibre that young couples used to have, and that 'commitment' was a word people don't seem to understand nowadays, by jove!, and that in our day (their day was considerably before our day, I might point out, but we were good enough or cowardly enough not to remind them of that) you made your promises and *jolly well stuck to them* through thick and thin, and all that stuff, and then Frank whatever-his-name-is said what he thought the real trouble was. The *real* trouble, he declared, was that the youngsters of today expected fireworks (meaningful nod to indicate that he was speaking of 'marital unpleasantness', as that character of Harry Enfield's calls it) all the way in their marriages, and gave up when it didn't happen. Surely, he inquired confidently, Mike would agree with him that such expectations were ridiculous.

"That was when Mike embarked on one of those little speeches of his that sceptics like us might suspect are designed to snuggle up to the good opinion of people he feels inferior to. They make my bones ache! Dip, it wouldn't have mattered if he'd just nodded and grunted something or other that sounded like a vague agreement – I mean, I don't really care what the posh Handleys think about our sex-life – but he didn't.

"'No,' said the style-king of the junior teaching world, the Oscar Wilde of Standham, swirling the brandy round in his glass and sipping with judicious consideration. 'I don't think you could describe what happens in a mature relationship as fireworks. No, Frank, I would say that long-term marriage is more like one of those wonderful, heavy old Aga cookers, wouldn't you, agree, Kathy? They last for years if you look after them properly, it's possible to get a really excellent glow going, and they produce really good meals as long as you give 'em a stoke every now and then.' Dip, this sherry is very expensive. If you're going to spit it all over the room I shan't give you any next time."

"I'm sorry!" spluttered Dip, "I really am. Give me some more. Gosh, I bet he wished he hadn't said that afterwards."

"Oh, yes, afterwards, you may bet your best cami-knickers on it. At the time, though, he just sat back and lapped up all the expensive, throaty sounds of merriment from Frank and Thingy Pooey Poshperson.

Then, in the car on the way home, he said it had really gone well, didn't I think? And I said, using my famous impression of a cucumber served after twenty-four hours in the freezer, 'I regret to announce that the heavy old Aga has gone out through consistent neglect and will require a complete service before it becomes functional again. Because of this there will certainly be no glowing tonight, and you need not expect any really good meals in the foreseeable future, stoke every now and then though you may,' and it was then that he began to realise I wasn't too impressed with his little flash of wit. Actually, we did laugh about it next morning, but . . ."

"But it set you thinking."

"It was a sort of trigger, I suppose, Dip. I started to feel very sad and worried and panicky about getting old and everything winding down and feeling flat. I don't *want* to be a heavy old Aga that glows sometimes. I'm not interested in being one of those highly respected Christian women in suits, with kind-sad eyes who resisted temptation once for all the very best reasons and are in a sensible long-term relationship with no fireworks and have written a lent-book about it. I want some sparklers and some bangers and some rockets and some – some things you have to be very careful with because they could be dangerous. There's got to be at least an outside chance of getting your fingers burned, hasn't there?" I paused, sipping my sherry again and wondering how much more to say. "I started to feel as if there was a really big decision to be made."

"About what?"

"Well, at the risk of you thinking I've finally looped the loop, it was – well, I saw it like this. It was the decision about whether to burst like an exploding star or shape myself like a comfortable armchair. I didn't feel ready to get old and spend my time shaping myself into whatever other people wanted me to be. I really didn't want that. I wanted lots of other things. I wanted to go through those first stages of falling in love again, Dip, when you go for a walk and ordinary things like trees and buses and brick walls look shiny and vivid and textured and full of meaning. Do you remember that glorious, half-witted feeling?"

"I remember – "

"I wanted to turn up in some cafe on Saturday morning at ten-thirty with everything in me buzzing and tingling because I was going to meet someone I'd been dreaming about all night and dressing and making-up for since getting up. I wanted to walk along a riverbank under weeping willows in the autumn like Mike and I used to when we first discovered each other up at Durham, finding to our amazement, like all couples falling in love since the beginning of time, that we felt exactly the same about absolutely everything under the sun, wondering when it would be right to hold hands for the first time and whether he would kiss me when we got back to the halls, and worrying about not being able to do it properly and – and all those warm and fruity things. I sat up really late in the kitchen one hot summer night this year with all the doors open, feeling one of those magical warm breezes running right through the length of the house from front to back, just gently brushing my face. It was sad and lovely, and it filled me full of aching and longing for – for something or other. Do you know – ?"

I looked at my friend for a moment. How safe is it to say some things?

"Go on," said Dip, "you might as well spit it out."

"In case it's infected, you mean? Sorry. Sorry, it's just that I was embarrassed for a moment. It seems so ridiculous to be saying this sitting at home on a Saturday morning at eleven o'clock – but there've been times when I wanted to sneak off down to a pub in the next town and sit at the bar and have a couple of drinks and see if I got chatted up."

"That doesn't sound much like the 'wondering when it would be right to hold hands' sort of stuff that you were talking about."

Putting my glass down on the small table beside me, I clasped my hands tightly together as I tried to find the words to explain.

"Oh, Dip, it wasn't that I really did want some sordid encounter with a fifth-rate gigolo from Milton Keynes – always assuming there might be a fifth-rate gigolo in Milton Keynes who specialises in travelling down this way for sordid encounters with forty-nine-year-old mothers of three. And I'm not one for getting crushes on film-stars like that droopy girl we used to have in our group." I couldn't help laughing suddenly. "Honestly, Dip, can you imagine me taking on the role of resident *femme fatale* in the Dog and Duck on Friday nights? It isn't just about sex, you see, Mike and I have always got on pretty well in that area – well, most of the time, anyway – it's more about feeling special and sparkly and – and fancied. Do you know what I mean?...

"So, after I'd accused Mike of being boring this morning, and then admitted that my real fear was getting old and him thinking I was boring, it was like a boil bursting – no, that's horrible, it wasn't like that. It was like a bubble popping – no, as you were, it was definitely a boil. Anyway, whatever it was, bubble or boil, it burst, and after that we got more glutinously lovey-dovey than we've managed to be at that passionless time of the morning for ages. And Mike said why don't we celebrate the beginning of me being old by having a real old-fashioned sixties party with the right music and silly dancing in tiny spaces because the room is too crowded and all the other things we were talking about just now? And he has promised, a little worriedly, him being stuck with being who he is, that he will do his best to ensure that romance will blossom once again in our relationship."

●◆●

Stress Family Robinson – The Birthday Party

I KNOW WHAT
YOU'RE GOING TO SAY

It is possible to prevent genuine dialogue in marriage because we are so sure we know what the other person is going to say. It can happen in our relationship with God as well. Those of you who are in close relationships may recognise this particularly twisted attempt at communication.

WIFE: John, I've been thinking

HUSBAND: Mmmm....

W: I've made a decision

H: Uh-huh?

W: I'm going to stop work in September.

H: Well –

W: I know what you're going to say. How are we going to manage on one salary? Well we've done it before, and we'll do it again. We're far too extravagant anyway. It'll do us good.

H: I –

W: It's no good trotting out your line about, "How will you cope without holidays and little treats?" You saying that really infuriates me! You're virtually calling me a simple-minded bimbo, which, for your information, I certainly am not.

H: You –

W: Don't bother telling me I've got some secret reason for stopping work, either. I haven't, and frankly I take exception to your view of me as a devious self-seeking female.

H: Could we –

W: No, don't try to smooth me over. You can't call someone a neurotic simpleton and then make it all right with a few glib phrases. No doubt you'll claim you "didn't mean it". Well if you didn't mean it you shouldn't have said it! How would you feel if you'd come to me with a carefully thought-through plan and had it steam-rollered? Because that's what you've done.

H: I –

W: No, please don't insult my intelligence by denying it. I simply won't listen. You've had your say, and now it's my turn, or perhaps I don't get a turn? Well I'm going to take it anyway. I've told you I want to stop work, but you don't seem to hear me. Or rather you did hear me, but all you could do is go on and on in your usual way about holidays and treats and me not coping. Negative as ever! *You* don't agree so that's that.

H: Lets –

W: You don't have to say any more. I get the message. Well all right, I won't stop work! But just you bear in mind that it was you who bullied me into carrying on.

H: When –

W: It's useless trying to backtrack now. It's too late! "Keep slaving away." Those are your orders to the resident servant. Well, okay, I will. But I loathe you sometimes, and one day I'll find the words to tell you how much – if I ever get a word in edgeways, which is unlikely.

H: But –

W: I'm sorry, I don't want to hear any more. You may not have finished but I have! I'm going out! Goodnight!

H: *(after a puzzled pause)* If only I'd kept my mouth shut . . .

◆

Cabbages for the King

REVELATIONS

They say you never really stop worrying about your children. My experience is that they, whoever they are, are quite right. Back in *Sacred Diary* land Gerald is on the verge of communicating his plans for the future to two very nervous parents.

Friday 22 April

Gerald very quiet at dinner tonight. As we finished eating, he leaned back in his chair and said, "Any chance we could have a bit of a chat on Sunday evening?"

Anne and I froze, me with a piece of Cathedral Cheddar halfway to my mouth, she in the act of scraping scraps from one plate onto another. Knew we were both wondering the same thing – was Gerald intending to solve the mystery of his three months off work and the long walks and the occasional unexplained absences? Very slowly and casually brought my piece of cheese to its intended destination. Anne continued with her scraping, but went on absent-mindedly moving her knife across the plate for a few seconds after there was nothing left to scrape. Both so anxious not to over-react that neither of us said anything at all.

Gerald said, "Hello! Anyone out there? I know it wasn't the most dynamic of questions, but I'd appreciate even the briefest of replies – if it's not too much trouble, that is."

Anne and I immediately launched into high-pitched laughing, compensatory babbling mode. One of the things I really like about Anne is her vulnerability when it comes to anything important connected with Gerald. She's so wise and calm with everyone else, but with him it's different. I must tell her that sometime (perhaps).

Agreed to "chat" on Sunday evening.

Saturday 23 April

Went for a long walk over the hills with Richard today. Poor old chap finds it very difficult to communicate easily when real feelings are involved. Told me that he and Charles are getting on very well, although Charles is still adamant that the whole Christian "thing" is not for him. Felt like crying when Richard said that he'd privately repented before the Lord for piling religious expectations on his son instead of simply loving him.

Asked how Doreen was.

Richard said she's very angry and tight-lipped. Will hardly speak to Charles and blames just about everything on Anne and one or two other people in the church. Says he doubts if she'll continue her involvement with my support group.

"I wish," said Richard dolefully, "that we were like you and Anne and Gerald. You must feel so glad that Gerald's settled in his faith and everything."

Agreed automatically, then suddenly realised that for all I'm supposed to be so open about myself I very rarely share what's troubling me *now*. I suppose that's why so many Christian speakers only ever seem to have problems in the past. Told Richard about our forthcoming "chat" with Gerald and how nervous we both were. He was so pleased to have something to comfort *me* about. Prayed together on a wooden seat overlooking the valley, then strolled down to a little pub I know where they do the most *excellent* pint of bitter. I know heaven is different things for different people, but settling down into the corner of a pub with a pint and a friend takes some beating.

Can't get to sleep tonight. Find myself wondering, as I used to wonder in the past, whether I would ever have been able to offer Gerald as a sacrifice, like Abraham with Isaac. Funny to think about all those times in the past when I used to apologize to God for loving Gerald more than I loved Jesus. Couldn't and can't imagine choosing between them. I tell myself I don't have that problem now that I understand God a little bit better. Not quite sure though. Wonder if Gerald knows how much I love him. Don't suppose he does. Should say these things more perhaps.

Yes, and mmmmmmmmmmmmmmmmmmmmmmmmmmmmmmmmm mmmmmmmmmmmmmmmmmmmmmmmmmmmmmmmmmmmmmmmmmmmmm mmmmmmmmmmmmmmmm

Easter Sunday 24 April

Woke up at midnight last night to find that I'd stupidly nodded off with my finger on the "m" button of my portable word processor. Did thirty-five pages of 'm' before waking up. Deleted them and went back to sleep. Thought I'd leave a few in just to keep the record accurate. Anne says that this decision is my final qualification for long-term institutional care.

Sometimes think my word processor despises me. It says scathing things like: DO YOU REALLY WANT TO SAVE *THIS*?

Easter Sunday is my favourite service, I think. Anything seems possible on Easter Sunday. Come to think of it – I suppose anything's possible *because* of Easter Sunday.

Didn't want the service to end today. Didn't want the evening to come.

Tea predictably a rather tense meal this evening. Anne ate hardly anything.

"Let's leave the washing-up," Gerald suggested as we finished, looking at me because it was my turn. "You and Mum go through to the sitting-room, and I'll bring you a coffee."

Went down the hall to the sitting-room with Anne, feeling, for some reason, as if we were joint job-applicants who had lied in pursuit of the post for which we were about to be interviewed. All sorts of nightmare scenarios flitted through my mind as we sat neatly together on the settee. Tried to blank them off. Felt a shiver go through me as I heard him coming along the hall. Everything could change in the next five minutes.

Looked at Anne. She blew out a breath she'd been holding in for some time and said, "Well, then."

"Yes," I said, "just what I was thinking."

Gerald fussed around with our coffee for an unnecessarily long time before sitting down in the armchair facing us. Took a few sips from a glass of something that was definitely not coffee.

I said, in what was supposed to be a joky tone but came out like something from the darkest bits of Macbeth, "We're not going to need one of those, then, Gerald?"

"Well, I'm not sure," said Gerald without smiling. "You might, actually. Do you want me to get you one?"

"Please, Gerald," Anne was looking rather white, "please say what it is you have to say. I'm not very good at dentists' waiting rooms."

"Nor am I," I said, suddenly very much not wanting to hear what Gerald had to say. "When I was at college a little group of us who all hated the dentist got together and pledged that whenever one of us had to go to have a tooth out, at least one of the others would go with him or her to make it a bit more bearable. As far as I can remember, we called ourselves the Action Faction for Distraction from Reaction to Extraction, and we met – "

"Adrian," said Anne.

"Yes?"

"Please be quiet."

"Sorry."

"Right," said Gerald, "here we go then." He looked at us for a moment.

"What I have to say to you may come as a bit of a surprise. To be honest, it surprised me when – well, when it happened. Let me tell you what it isn't, just to put your minds at rest. For instance, I'm not gay."

Anne and I fell about laughing on the sofa. Gay indeed! As if we'd ever worried about such a thing! What a hoot! In any case we have a warmly compassionate view of such things, so we'd have handled it, wouldn't we?

Breathed an inward sigh of relief. Nightmare scenario number one out of the way, thank God.

"Nor am I pregnant," said Gerald solemnly.

Well, this *was* turning out to be a jolly session! Not pregnant – ha, ha, ha!

"Nor have I impregnated anybody else."

Phew! That was n.s. number two disposed of. Perhaps it wouldn't be anything very alarming after all. Perhaps it was just going to be –

"I'm going to be a male stripper," said Gerald.

Sat and stared in utter amazement. Hurriedly scanned my list of nightmare scenarios. Not a male stripper in sight.

I said, "Gerald, I'm absolutely –"

"Adrian," interrupted Anne, "I think that might have been a joke, don't you?"

"Sorry, Dad," said Gerald penitently, "finding it a bit tricky coming to the point." He cleared his throat. "It's about my faith, actually."

Found myself harking back nostalgically to those dear distant days, a few seconds ago, when I'd thought my only son was planning to make a living as a male stripper. After all, what was so very wrong with taking your clothes off in public? Found myself pleading silently with God:

"Don't let it be that Gerald doesn't believe anything any more. All those nights when he was little – you must remember how I'd creep into his bedroom when he was asleep and talk to you about him – ask you, sometimes with tears in my eyes, to look after him and keep him close to you? That was a prayer, and you answer prayer, don't you? Don't you?"

"Do you remember, Dad," said Gerald, "that time when Father John came to speak at the church and said heaven would have to involve some cricket just for you?"

"Mmm." I nodded and smiled, remembering that particular service very well indeed. It had solved a long-standing problem for me.

"Well, at coffee time afterwards I was having a bit of a chat with him, and he said, right out of the blue, 'Ever thought that you might end up in the Anglican ministry?' I didn't know what to say, so I suppose I was a bit flippant. I said that, firstly, I didn't really know what the Anglican Church was; secondly, I hadn't got anything to preach; and thirdly, God was still a complete mystery to me. He laughed and said, 'In that case you precisely fulfil the normal qualifications. In fact,

I'm pretty sure that, if he was here now, the bishop would ordain you on the spot.' I thought it was quite funny at the time, but I certainly didn't take it very seriously. Over the years, though – it's funny really – I've heard Father John's voice asking me that question in my mind over and over again. It's been like a sort of pointless secret that's not worth sharing with anyone else, but then, one Sunday about a year ago, I went to this Anglican church just up the road from where I was living. I'd been there a few times before, actually, but I don't really know why. It wasn't particularly lively, and the vicar looked kind of defeated. I knew he must be feeling threatened by his congregation the first time I went there – I mean, you're supposed to begin your sermon with 'Dearly beloved', aren't you, not 'Ladies and gentlemen of the jury'?"

I tittered dutifully, filled with relief that my son was neither gay nor pregnant nor about to become the unscheduled male stripper. Anne didn't laugh. She clicked her tongue impatiently.

"Sorry, Mumsy," said Gerald, "silly joke – bit embarrassed. I was sitting in the evening service on this particular Sunday, my presence probably having lowered the average age of the congregation to about eighty-three, and I'd just been asking myself what on earth I thought I was doing there, when a sort of feeling went through me. That's the only way I can describe it – like a beam of light filling me up and passing on, but – but leaving behind a quiet sort of sureness that I was going to end up ..."

Gerald didn't seem to be quite able to finally say the words.

"Say it, Gerald," said Anne.

"I heard that same question again, even clearer than before – just the same words, except that this time it wasn't Father John asking, and this time I said 'Yes'. I think God was asking me to become a priest in the Anglican Church. I know one or two people would attack me with several specially sharpened chunks of Scripture for saying that, but that's their problem, I'm afraid. I don't mean that nastily, but I sure as eggs do mean it.'

Anne said, "Of course."

"So, over the last few months," continued Gerald, "I've been walk-ing and thinking and praying and doing bits of writing for you, Dad, and just checking that I've not got carried away by my own imagination. I was sure before, but I'm even surer now. That's what I'm going to do, and I've been to see the director of thingamabobs and set the whole thing in motion." He smiled at us as he's been smiling at us for twenty-four years. "What do you think?"

Finished the bottle of not-coffee between us.

• ◆ •

Sacred Diary of Adrian Plass, Christian Speaker,
Aged Forty-Five and Three Quarters

UNDERSTANDING
THE DANCE

Divine messages or parables can be slipped into the most unlikely, family-related activities. God has certainly used this creative and sometimes amusing way of communicating with Bridget and me over the years

> With many such parables he spoke the word to them, as they
> were able to hear it; he did not speak to them except in parables,
> but he explained everything in private to his disciples.
>
> Mark 4 : 33–34 NRSV

Here in these two verses we discover a collection of words that should, in my not very humble opinion, be displayed on the bathroom mirror and screen-saver and filofax cover of every man or woman who has any intention of talking to people about the things of God. Jesus spoke to the people in nothing but parables. In parables only did he speak to the people. The people heard only parables from Jesus. Parables alone did the people hear from Jesus. Are you getting tired of me saying that? I repeat it in all its permutations because some of us may still be missing the point.

Jesus might have had a variety of motives for approaching his ministry in this way, but there was one overwhelming reason for using stories. No prizes for guessing. People liked stories. They enjoyed listening to stories. They were likely to remember the content and point of stories. Indeed, so entertained, absorbed and fascinated were they by some of these stories that, on at least two occasions, thousands of them forgot all about the need to organise lunch and ended up sitting on a hillside feeling hungry (fortunately for them, Jesus was as sensitive to physical requirements as he was to spiritual need).

How have we managed to lose sight of the fact that, in this respect, people do not and probably never will change? Somewhere on the long, strangely winding road between the years when Jesus walked the Earth and the present day, a view must have developed in some quarters that the content of preaching and teaching should be more or less on a par with nasty medicine. You don't like it, but you've got to take it and swallow it for your own good. It doesn't matter if it's boring as long as it's worthy. Dull acquiescence to an hour and a half of grey, turgid, incontrovertible truth is just what you need to keep your faith fizzing along.

I ask you! What possible merit can there be in an irksome and unvarying diet of thick porridge without salt or sweetness, that will just about keep you alive but make you wish you weren't? Please don't misunderstand me, by the way. Not for one moment am I suggesting that people should not be challenged and made to face up to hard truths. Many of the parables that Jesus told had exactly that effect on those who heard them. Imagine it:

"So, who is my neighbour?" asks an expert on the law, hoping to catch the Master out.

"Well," says Jesus, "a certain man was going down from Jerusalem to Jericho ..."

The story of violence and neglect and compassion that we know so well begins and continues. Soon the expert is so engrossed that his original question has flown from his grown-up head like a migrating bird. He is a child listening to a tale.

"So," says Jesus as the story ends, "which of these three do you think was a neighbour to the man who fell into the hands of robbers?"

"The one who had mercy on him, of course."

It was a prompt reply. But after that? Did the expert on the law experience something of an inner shock as it dawned on him that the outcome of the verbal three-card trick he had just witnessed was more revealing of himself than of Jesus?

No, the technique of teaching through stories certainly doesn't let anyone off the hook. Quite often parables entertain us at the front door while the truth creeps in through a side-window and sandbags us on the back of the head.

There are some first-class storytellers around, but we need more. Let's pray that more will arise. Let's encourage them. Let's be them. Let's not be boring. Let's not put up with being bored.

It is also worth mentioning that parables are by no means limited to stories told by public speakers. If we look out for them we may well spot parables in our own daily experiences, events, or situations that contain within them a message or signpost for the direction of our lives.

Here is a rather obvious one from my own life.

It happened when I had spent most of one week in a place overflowing with passion and high drama, a place where one was able to witness starbursts of joy and floods of tears. It was a place where dreams were being fulfilled and hearts were being broken, where one could see the best and the worst of what it means to be human. I had seen scorn and encouragement, compassion and vindictiveness, bitterness and courage, optimism and the final demise of hope.

What place was this where tragedy battled with delight? Perhaps some sad, war-torn corner of a distant land, where unsung heroes battled hideous giants of callousness and exploitation?

No, it was the local Dance Festival in which my thirteen-year-old daughter was taking part. I don't know if you are familiar with events like this, but if you are, and you have endured them, I know you will have no wish to read on. To have such memories stirred would depress you, so do feel free to move on to the next bit of this book. We'll catch you up in a minute.

For those who have never experienced the above phenomenon, I'll try to explain.

You are in a large hall or theatre with a wide stage at one end. In the centre aisle of the auditorium, close to the stage, stands a raised dais on which two chairs and a table have been placed. This is where the adjudicator and her assistant sit in order to have a good view of the performances. The adjudicator is responsible for awarding a mark to each child in each class.

There are many classes. They include Modern, Tap, Ballet, Greek, Song and Dance, National, Improvisation, and other categories that have been blessedly wiped from my memory. The number of children appearing in each class varies. Two of the ones I had to sit through in the course of that week seemed to involve several hundred children and take several days to complete, but that may not have been an entirely reliable or sane judgement.

One of the things that produced such warped assessments was the fact that a bewilderingly high number of these solo dances appeared to be identical. The titles were different. In fact, now that I think about it, the titles were the *most* different thing about them.

In the Character class that I watched for a month or two on one of the days, for instance, the monotonous, amplified voice from behind the curtain announced, "Mary Jones, dancing 'The River'. The river flows from the mountains down to the sea".

This was the cue for Mary Jones to appear on stage, where she hopped about and ran around for a bit being a river flowing down to the sea.

"Next," declared the dispassionate amplified voice, "Nicola Edwards, dancing 'The Shepherdess'. The girl who tends the flock belonging to her master goes off to search for a lost lamb and returns only to find that a wolf is attacking the rest of the flock. She fights off the wolf, and then, though fatally injured herself, she returns the sheep to her master, who mourns her as she dies in his arms."

Enter Nicola Edwards, who hops about and runs around for a bit in order to represent this entire depressing chain of events.

Another thirty-two children do the same.

Behind the adjudicator sit the parents, once they have finished plastering their children with make-up and encasing them in their costumes round behind the stage. And it is in this group that you would have found the high tension and dramatic sweep of emotions that I have already described. The emotional heat on this occasion was simply indescribable, not least in parental attitudes to the female adjudicator.

Those whose children had been given high marks were deeply, warmly appreciative of her perceptive qualities and wise judgement. In fact, they felt that she was rather an exceptional woman. By contrast, mothers whose little girls had failed to score well were shocked and scandalised by some unknown idiot's lunatic decision to trust this blind, incompetent, spiteful, artistically barren, probably corrupt individual with the task of allotting marks to their sensitive, gifted offspring . . .

Interestingly, as far as this matter of performances all being similar is concerned, my own daughter's entry in the Greek class on the Thursday was markedly distinct from *all* the others. Additionally, I was able to take a totally objective view of the adjudicator's judgement in awarding my daughter a very high mark in that same class. She was indeed an *exceptional* woman. Why things should have been so very different solely in the case of myself and my own daughter, I really could not say.

That was my immediate perception of events.

Reality hit me a little later, of course, and if you and I fail to understand the parable contained within this little account we really don't deserve to hear any more stories.

* ⬥ *

Never Mind the Reversing Ducks

DEAR DADDY

The Unlocking includes some tough questions, including doubts about being spiritually organised enough to say any prayers that God could possibly want to hear.

So, how do we communicate with God? Out of the mouths ...

———

> For you did not receive a spirit that makes you a slave again to fear, but you received a Spirit of sonship. And by him we cry, "Abba, Father".
>
> Romans 8 : 15

When Bob Hope was asked if he thought he would be going to heaven he replied, "Well, I sure hope I don't miss out on a technicality."

A lot of the people that I meet have exactly that problem. What if their theology is deficient in some crucial area? Will the keeper of heaven's gate scan their personal statement of faith and, with a regretful shake of the head, announce that they've not quite made it, in the same way that a driving test is failed because of one trivial error? Theology maintains the purity of the divine stream, but love is the boat that carries us to Jesus. Katy, age six, sent a letter to me when I was touring South Africa on my own in 1993. It was a message from a child to her father, and it contains some interesting features.

She began by expressing her hope that I would write to her when I got to South America. Appalling, don't you think? I wasn't in South America, was I? I was in South Africa. At the bottom of the letter she drew a picture that was supposed to look like me. As a so-called representation of my face it was wildly inaccurate (anyone who thinks otherwise is in serious trouble).

Then there was the spelling. At least two mistakes. Since when was "sposto" included in the *Oxford Dictionary*? There were three crossings out, and as for the lines of handwriting – well, they were all over the place, up and down like a roller-coaster. It looked as if she'd been standing in a quicksand when she wrote them. And what had happened to the address and the date and the telephone number? They weren't there, were they? Lots of kisses, but they don't tell you anything useful, do they? What kind of communication *was* this?

I'll tell you what kind of communication this was. It was the most wonderful letter any lonely father ever had from a beloved child. Do you seriously think that I would have wanted so much as a single letter to be changed, just for the sake of some boring, legalistic accuracy? No, of course not. Every kiss counted. Each tongue-protruding attempt to convey love touched my heart in that distant, troubled land.

Theology is important, but God needs to be loved like everyone else. Don't be afraid to climb onto his knee because you lack understanding. Daddies need kisses, and the rest can wait.

If you really want to communicate with God, remember Kate's letter.

• ◆ •

The Unlocking

Part Three

PATTERNS

Patterns, conscious or unconscious, are essentially neutral, aren't they? In family life, as in any other situation, they can be helpful, destructive, or even a bewildering combination of both. The fact that in some cases they can make us laugh and in others reduce us to tears, suggests that they might be well worth taking a look at. Let's do that. Here are some examples

THE GREAT
PACKING DEBATE

One of the most puzzling things for the average child must be the way in which their parents not only construct arguments out of nothing but actually repeat the same module of conflict every time a particular situation arises.

Many arguments have tunes, and, in some cases, my wife Bridget and I have been playing the same pieces of music for more than thirty years now. Like two professional actors in some long-running play we step almost automatically into our roles and embark on the script that we have come to know so well during the course of our marriage. Fortunately, again like actors, we conclude most of these performances with a friendly chat and a drink or two.

Of course, when the music of conflict becomes too agonizingly discordant, something has to change, but most of our oft-repeated rows are like comfortable old shoes. An example? Well, take the whole business of Packing.

Bridget and I both claim to know exactly how packing should be done. My method is neat, logical and takes about three days. Hers is wild, unfathomable and takes about three hours. I feel quite sure that the time factor in my method could be significantly improved if we only gave it a chance. But we never do. I always retire in fury after a few minutes and sulk somewhere while Bridget does it her way. The dialogue that precedes my walk-out usually goes something like this:

A: (*with totally unconvincing casualness*) Right, well, we might as well get started on the packing, then.

B: Darling, wouldn't you rather do something with the children while I –

A: Why don't we try to be really systematic this time.

B: (*groans*) Oh, no . . .

A: We've got six cases altogether, right?

B: What was wrong with the way we did it last time?

A: Nothing – much. It's just that I can't get involved when you organize it. We end up in a sea of clothes and shoes and books and bits and pieces with the cases buried somewhere underneath, and I wade dismally through it all with a tea cloth in my hand wondering where it fits into your master-plan. I don't know where anything is, I don't know where anything goes, I dunno what's going on, and I –

B: And you start shaking your head and sighing and rolling your eyes up into the top of your head like some bad Victorian actor and talking about how your bad childhood makes it difficult for you to cope with chaos.

A: I don't do that.

B: You're almost doing it now, and we haven't even started yet.

A: (*with what he considers to be heroic self-control*) Look, all I'm saying is that we could *try* it my way and just see how we get on – just try it, for goodness sake!

B: Your way being what, exactly? (*she knows*)

A: (*as if explaining to an imbecile*) Right! We take all six cases out into the garden. Right?

B: (*nodding wearily*) And we put them in a nice neat row –

A: We put them in a row – it doesn't have to be that neat a row – with the lids open, and we number them from one to five, and agree about what sort of luggage is going into each one, then we bring stuff out from the house bit by bit and fill the cases one by one until there's nothing left in the house that's supposed to be in the cases. Apart from anything else it would be so much more fun doing it this way. You'd say to me, "Here's a shirt, Adrian, it goes in number three," and I'd go out and put it in number three. Then you might say, "Here's a pair of shoes, Adrian, they go in number five, so I put them in number five and come back for the next thing, and so on. Then we could swoop round and I'd say, "Here's a blouse, Bridget –"

B: (*mimicking*) It goes in number four . . .

A: (*refusing to be put off*) And you'd go out and put it in number four, then you'd come back for the next thing and so on. Then, when everything's in, we shut the cases – one, two, three, four, five! – and that's that. The packing's done, everything's ready and we haven't had to hack our way through forests of underwear and overcoats just to find the floor. *(pause)* How can you say that that doesn't make sense? How can it possibly *not* make sense? How? Well, how can it? Come on – tell me how that can possibly *not* make sense! It seems so obvious –

B: Adrian, I wish to make the following observations. First of all, let us calmly consider the difference between your method and mine. Your method may be neat and logical, but it would take – ooh – about a year to get everything packed. In fact, it would become more of a hobby than a functional task. My method, on the other hand, may appear wild and unfathomable and cause you unspeakable anguish, but it would mean the packing gets done before we leave for America – an attractive little feature of my approach, wouldn't you say? Furthermore, touched though I am by the pretty picture you paint of you and me trotting happily and eternally to and fro with shirts and blouses and pairs of shoes, I have no intention of playing "Jane And John Go On Their Holidays" out in the garden just to pander to your completion neurosis. *You* may not know what's going on when I'm packing, but I do. And as it's always me that ends up doing it anyway, that's all that really matters, isn't it? Why don't you go for a walk or play golf or whatever you like, and by the time you come back the work will be done and you won't have to worry about it. How does that sound?

A: *(sensing an opportunity to be deeply hurt and play golf)* Are you saying you don't want me to help?

B: Of course I'd like you to help – if you really mean it. What I can't stand is having you huffing and puffing around and getting irritable about not being able to do anything while I'm busy doing it.

A: *(deciding to be offended)* Oh, well, in that case, I might just as *well* go and play golf, or perhaps you think I won't be able to organize *that*! *(slams out)*

B: *(counting on her fingers)* One, two, three, four –
A: *(reappearing)* Err, have you seen my clubs . . . ?

•—◆—•

Adapted from *Stress Family Robinson* for performance

NICE

The "Nice" sketch, from *Clearing Away the Rubbish*, is a rather alarmingly raw slice of life. It involves a married couple, well practised in the art of tearing each other to pieces, battling doggedly along one of their familiar argumentative ruts.

When Bridget and I perform this sketch, we find that it touches people and provokes response on a number of levels, especially in the case of married couples. It has no visible Christian content, but I think that's the whole point. Many married Christian couples simply cannot understand why they experience such intense and even violent conflict in a relationship which "should" be loving and peaceful. This sketch offers no answers, but it might, like a benevolent grenade, explode some of the resistance people quite naturally feel to the idea of opening up to others who might be able to help.

If you want to have a go at acting out "Nice" in your own church or group, bear in mind that it requires some acting skill and careful direction. Ideally it's performed in a pool of light. The only other things required are a suitcase, which is being packed with clothes by the man as the sketch proceeds, and a single chair. Don't worry about laughs at the beginning of the sketch. They soon fade!

(Man is packing. Woman is watching.)

WOMAN: Why are you going?

MAN: I've had enough.

WOMAN: Enough of what?

MAN: Enough of you.

WOMAN: Enough of me what?

MAN: Enough of you asking me what I've had enough of.

WOMAN: You must have had enough of some thing.

(Pause)

What have you had enough of?

MAN: Well, if you must know, I've had enough of you being nice.

WOMAN: But what's . . . ?

MAN: And loving, and generous, and forgiving, and . . . clean.

WOMAN: What's wrong with being lov – all those things?

MAN: The thing that's wrong with being all those things is that I'm not. I'm unpleasant, hateful, mean, unforgiving, and scruffy.

WOMAN: No, you're not.

MAN: Yes, I am.

WOMAN: No, you're not.

MAN: (Loudly) Yes, I am!

WOMAN: Well . . . maybe you are.

MAN: No, I'm not!

WOMAN: You just said you were.

MAN: Well, I'm allowed to say I am. You're too nice to agree with me.

WOMAN: But you just said you didn't like me being nice.

MAN: No, I did not.

WOMAN: You did.

MAN: I didn't.

WOMAN: You did!

MAN: I did not. I said I'd had enough of you being nice. I have had sufficient. Thank you for supplying me with an appropriate amount of niceness. I have now had enough. I have packed all your niceness with my socks and shirts and underwear, and I am going to find someone or somewhere that will supply me with an equal amount of something else that I have not got enough of.

WOMAN: It's not fair.

MAN: Thank you for being so understanding.

WOMAN: I meant it's not fair to me.

MAN: But I just told you – I don't do fair things. You are fair. I am unfair. You are a very wonderful person, I am slightly less wonderful than a turd.

WOMAN: Don't be silly.

MAN: I am also silly.

WOMAN: You're being ridiculous.

MAN: And ridiculous.

WOMAN: What you really mean is that I never give you an excuse for doing the things you've really wanted to do since about two weeks after we got married! You'd like me to be really nasty so that you can storm out and sulk with some sympathetic stray female and moan to her about me not understanding you.

(*Pause*)

MAN: That's not very nice. That is not very nice at all. I have never, never, ever, ever heard you talk like that before. Never!

(*Pause*)

WOMAN: Look, I didn't mean any of that. It's not true really. I'm sorry. Please forgive me.

MAN: (*She must be joking*) Oh, yes it is! You meant every single word. And that's why I'm leaving. Because you think I want you to give me an excuse for doing things that you claim I've really wanted to do since about two weeks after we got married, and that I'd like you to be really nasty so that I can storm out and sulk with some sympathetic stray female and moan to her about you not understanding me. I mean – just how nasty can you get?

(*She cries*)

I even have to do my own packing!

WOMAN: (*Eagerly*) Let me do it for you! I'd like to . . .

MAN: No-o-o thanks. I'd rather do it myself.

(*Pause*)

Very nice of you to offer, though. Very nice.

WOMAN: But I still don't understand what I've done wrong!

MAN: You've done nothing wrong, that's what you've done wrong. Deliberately and with malice aforethought, you have set out to do nothing wrong. You are an incurable, incorrigible grown-up, and I am the miserable means by which you train and strengthen the muscles of your horrible maturity. You club me with tolerant wisdom, castrate me with forgiveness, and drown me in niceness. You are unmercifully loving. I am getting smaller and smaller and smaller every day. I am running out of ways to bully you or make you sorry for me. I am tired of waiting for you to do something fundamentally mean or vicious or disloyal, and I'm not going to wait any longer. I would like to add, though, that throughout everything, you have been unfailingly – nice.

(*Pause*)

WOMAN: (*Touches him*) You won't really go. You just wanted to work yourself up so that you could say all that. It's gone now. You won't really go.

(*Long pause*)

MAN: You're absolutely right, of course. I won't really go. I never do go, do I? I expect I just – wanted to say all that.

WOMAN: Why don't we just forget about it?

(*Pause*)

I'll unpack for you.

(*Pause*)

Then I'll cook us a nice dinner.

MAN: And you promise you'll try to be just a little nastier?

WOMAN: (*She means it*) I'll do anything that makes you happy, darling. I promise.

MAN: Well, that's very – very nice of you. Very nice.

(*She starts to unpack*)

●—◆—●

Clearing Away the Rubbish

SUNDAY LUNCH

Here's another pattern. This time it's Sunday lunch, a bit of an institution in British homes, as I believe it is in many other countries of the world. The intended pattern is, of course, one of familial togetherness and harmony. The reality can fall quite a long way short of this sparkling ideal.

The extract used here is adapted from Book Two in the *Stress Family Robinson* series. Kathy tells the story.

"Mum, when's dinner going to be ready?"

"It's ready now, Mark, but we are not having it until Felicity's done her violin practise, so speak to her, not me. I'm sick of telling her. She promised to do it last night, but she watched something instead. She said it would be all right because she'd do it before church today and she didn't do it. Then she promised to do it as soon as we got back, but she still didn't do it. She can jolly well do it now or nobody's going to eat today. And you can get the glasses out."

"Why are you speaking as if you're cross with me?"

"I'm not cross with you, I'm cross with Felicity."

"Felicity! Come and do your – oh, it's all right, Mum, Dip's helping her."

"Fine, but as a matter of trivial detail, I haven't heard any violin playing yet. Call me a slave to habit, but I've rather got into the way of expecting to hear the violin being played when a practise is in progress. Get the glasses out."

"What's Jack doing, then?"

"I can't hear you over the violin. What did you say?"

"I asked you what Jack's doing?"

"Are you eighteen or four?"

"How many?"

"Six with Dip."

"Can I have mine on my lap? I'm going out at half-past two."

"You'll have to change your trousers if you're going to have your dinner on your lap. No, you can't."

"No funnier than last time or the time before that, Mum. Can't we start?"

"Tell everyone to come, and we'll start as soon as Felicity's been through Vivaldi a couple of times, if Vivaldi can stand it."

A few minutes later Mark bellowed, "DINNER, EVERYONE!"

"*I* could have done that, Mark!"

"Why did you ask me to, then?"

Sunday lunch-times in our house had been many things over the last couple of decades. When the children were small Mike often talked about how much he was looking forward to future years when these richly traditional occasions would be spiced with good conversation and bright convivial laughter, weekly opportunities for the cementing of good family relationships, and the healing of any small rifts that might have occurred during the previous week. A ripple of mildly hysterical inner laughter passes through me when I think of those projections now. As far as I can recall, Mike's charmingly civilised scenario did not allow for such phenomena as two brothers making determined efforts to batter each other's heads in with place-mats in a vicious argument over the last roast potato, nor a wildly irrational wife and mother sending a bowl of steaming hot leeks skating down the length of the table like a curling stone after two of her family had made being-sick noises as soon as the lid was removed, these being two of the more dramatic highlights that sprang immediately to mind. Nor, to my recollection, was there any awareness in those sweet innocent days before the children excitedly discovered God's wonderful gift of free will, that simply getting all of them to sit down at the table at the same time would so often prove to be a task of considerable magnitude.

As a result, Sunday lunch was traditionally a rather tense occasion in our house, precisely (ludicrously, when one thought about it) because everyone was aware that Mike so wanted it to be relaxed. Five people more or less busting a gut to produce a family idyll that never had really existed in the first place is hardly conducive to relaxation. The best times had always been when Dip was there, not because the children were on their reluctant best behaviour with a visitor – as a matter of history, they weren't – but because she had that hot-water-bottley sort of presence that seems to so successfully combat the chilling draughts of ill-grace and dispute. Even more important, perhaps, was the very special rapport that existed between her and Mark, whose usual idea of an enjoyable lunch was to get the food down his neck and clear off as soon as we acceded to his mumbled request to be allowed to "get down". When Dip was with us he actually seemed to want to be there.

She was with us today.

As soon as Felicity had played through her piece for a third time and been sent back to put her violin away, the six of us assembled around our long kitchen table (my favourite piece of furniture, by the way) and Mike began to carve the joint.

"Right!" he said contentedly as he carved. "How about someone suggesting a really nice family activity for this afternoon, something we can all do together for a change?"

As he spoke the first plate was in the process of being passed to the other end of the table, where Mark distracted anyone who might have been about to answer this question by drawing back in apparent terror at the sight of the generous slices on his plate.

"This is unlucky meat!" he exclaimed, his voice trembling like one of those gloriously talent-free actors in the early horror movies.

"And why might that be?" enquired Mike calmly, continuing to saw placidly.

"Please," groaned Jack, "I don't think we really want to know, do we?"

Felicity wanted to know. She always wanted to know everything.

"Why is it unlucky meat, Mark?"

"Because," replied Mark in sepulchral tones, "this is the lamb that gambolled and lost."

"O-o-oh, good," said Jack Blackadderishly, apparently greatly relieved, "I was only worried that it might turn out to be a bad joke, but as it's not a joke at all, that's fine."

Felicity's frowning gaze was still fixed on Mark.

"Gambled at what?"

"Not gambled – gambolled! Gambolled sounds like betted but it means skipped about."

Felicity looked doubtfully at the plate of meat that had by now appeared in front of her, another more troubled question framing itself on her lips.

"It's not funny when you have to explain it," complained Mark as he passed the vegetables to his sister.

"Don't worry," said Jack kindly, "it's not funny when you don't have to explain it as well."

"Violin seems to be going very well."

Dip's bright comment was obviously designed to distract Felicity from the mental image of the collected source of our various dinners skipping happily around a field in its original state.

She nodded, and Mike said, "Yes, she's really come on lately. You're doing quite difficult pieces now, aren't you, Darling?"

It was true. Felicity had begun to learn the violin a few years ago, by a Japanese method that demanded the presence of a parent at all lessons. The wretchedly unmusical but available parent in this case had been me. As the weeks went by, I had begun to feel rather like a junior school child myself in my abject fear that Mr Tyson, Felicity's violin teacher, would tell me off if I arrived late for the lesson each Wednesday morning, or if my daughter had demonstrably not practised since the last time. Early in this lengthy learning process the whole family had become accustomed to gritting their teeth and finding ways to survive endless, squeaky repetitions of "Twinkle, twinkle, little star" in a greater variety of musical forms than it seemed possible for the mind of man or woman to devise. As time went by, though, Felicity's skill increased dramatically, and now her fingers fairly flew up and down the neck of her three-quarter-size instrument.

The trickiest aspect of it all, no one will be surprised to hear, was getting her to practise. My arsenal in this on-going warfare consisted of encouragement, threats, bribes, the occasional parental sulk, fury, flattery, shouting very loudly, coaxing very gently, making her cry, making her laugh, and presenting her with cosmically awful, end-of-the-world-as-we-know-it alternatives. Jack's idea was the one that worked longest and best. He suggested putting a small sweet or trinket under an upturned cup in the practise area and letting Felicity have it when the session was finished. This device, one of the many ploys I would have scorned in those dear sweet days when children were purely hypothetical, really appealed to her, and got us through the most difficult patch of all. Nowadays she still had to be pressured into practising, but her music really did seem to have become part of who she was. She could actually *play* the violin, and even enjoy it. My daughter could play the *violin*! I was amazed every time I thought about it.

"Felicity," said Jack, "could I ask you a question about your violin music? There's something that's been puzzling me."

Felicity looked suspiciously at her oldest brother as he poured gravy over the pile of food on his plate. Jack's jokes always started very seriously.

"What about it?"

"You see, I had the idea that usually at the top of a sheet of music, it says something like 'Sprightly, with an air of freedom', or 'Loudly, and with passion', something like that. Don't they usually say something of that sort?"

"Might do. Dunno. Why?"

"Well, your music is quite different from that, isn't it? I noticed at the top of one of them it says, 'Reluctantly, and with an air of resentment', and on the other one it says, 'Morosely, and with little grunting sounds of annoyance.' Perhaps that's why you've found practising so difficult. You're following the instructions too closely."

Felicity speared a piece of hot roast potato, popped it in her mouth, and spoke through and round it with exaggerated, compensatory clarity.

109

"You and Mark should go and tell your sad jokes about skipping sheep and things at the top of music to some people who are fed up with laughing and want to have a serious time for a while."

"Don't eat with your mouth full, Felicity," I corrected automatically. "What are you all laughing about? Oh – you knew what I meant."

• ◆ •

Stress Family Robinson – The Birthday Party

LEAVE IT!

Another *Stress Family* extract. Kathy and Mike are fascinated observers of an incident that highlights the way in which patterns of authority structure can unconsciously develop in the most ordinary family.

Mike and I were sitting on one of the old wrought-iron Victorian seats on our local common one summer afternoon.

A family of four, out for an afternoon stroll, passed us on the satisfyingly elegant tree-lined avenue that runs along the south edge of the common and the cricket-pitch. Dad was in the lead, looking faintly bored and exasperated, yet, at the same time, very responsible and Dad-like. He carried a long, whippy stick in his hand, ready to slash at brambles and beat off any bush monsters that might leap from the undergrowth to attack his wife or his little brood. Half of his little brood followed a few yards behind, a pigtailed girl of about ten, full of oldest-child confidence, leading with her chin and chest, marching along rather than walking. Next came Mum, dressed in precisely the clothes you wear for walking on the common, an exact but larger copy of her daughter, the two of them looking like a couple of those hollow dolls that fit into each other, but with two or three stages left out. The other half of the brood, obviously the youngest in the family, and certainly lowest in the pecking-order as far as this particular little familial farm-yard was concerned, was a boy of around six years old, who, at this stage of the walk, had stopped to explore the invitingly accessible lower branches of a horse-chestnut. He was now dangling contentedly by both hands from the lowest branch of the tree, waiting, as small boys so healthily and enviably do, for the next thing to happen.

The next thing to happen was Dad realising that his small son was lagging behind and deciding it was time he caught up.

"Leave it!"

Sometimes we parents issue orders to our small children with a military sharpness and acidity that we would never dream of using with anyone else. Fortunately, the extent to which small children respond and give credence to this sort of excess tends to be in directly inverse proportion to the degree of sharpness and acidity injected into the command. Children may be inexperienced, but they're not silly. They seem to be aware at a very early age that, in the mechanics of obedience, frequency invariably outweighs vocal force. That explains why this typical specimen of a small boy continued to dangle happily from his branch despite the parental admonition. He was still a long way from having to do what he was told, and he knew it.

"Leave it!!"

This time Dad slammed the phrase out like a man hammering a second nail into stubbornly hard wood after bending the first one, and with much greater force than he had used on the first attempt. Innocent folk who never were part of such a family might have assumed quite reasonably at this point that it was bound to do the trick. Such crashing dominance, such threateningly fierce tones, must surely result in the lad instantly dropping to the ground and rushing like the wind to catch up with his father to apologize before some dreadful punishment befell him. Touching naïveté! He continued to dangle, of course.

It was Mum's turn.

"LEAVE IT!"

The sheer venom with which the lad's mother screeched exactly the same pair of words as her mate would have been deeply alarming if Mike and I had not been so aware of the previously mentioned frequency/force equation. Mike whispered that he would have moved like a shot if she'd spoken to him like that, but the little boy we were observing with such interest was possessed of crucial, family-related information. He knew exactly what he was doing. He continued to dangle – and as he dangled, he grinned.

"Leave it!"

This fourth and, as it transpired, final command was transmitted in a lordly squeak by our little hero's sister – she who, at this stage of their lives at any rate, was probably his greatest enemy on the face of the earth. Knowing her power, she had not even bothered to turn her head as she spoke. Gloriously unhampered by the civilised restraints that might have curbed her parents in dealing with their smallest offspring, this girl would be capable, at the correct, expertly judged moment, of doing her brother surgically precise harm when she next encountered him in that unpoliced jungle of a world that is called "When the grown-ups are not about".

Four identical directives had been issued, culminating in the boy's worst enemy entering the fray. Clearly, he felt that it was time for the force of gravity to be strategically employed. Dropping lightly to the ground, he scampered to catch the others up – still grinning.

All families are the same, with varying degrees of sophistication. They have their own special, private sets of rules and their own ways of playing out the same old set-pieces again and again, often in a virtually identical way, not necessarily as a result of being blinkered, but simply because they are *them*.

•◆•

Stress Family Robinson – The Birthday Party

TEMPLATES

Strong patterns, or templates, established in early life can have surprisingly long-term effects. Here is an example from *Never Mind the Reversing Ducks*.

> As Jesus passed along the Sea of Galilee, he saw Simon and his brother Andrew casting a net into the sea – for they were fishermen.
>
> And Jesus said to them, "Follow me and I will make you fish for people."
>
> And immediately they left their nets and followed him. As he went a little farther, he saw James son of Zebedee and his brother John, who were in their boat mending the nets. Immediately he called them; and they left their father Zebedee in the boat with the hired men, and followed him.
>
> Mark 1 : 16 – 20 NRSV

Nowadays people seem to change careers quite often, don't they? But I am quite sure that Simon and Andrew and James and John never dreamed that the future could hold anything but fishing – for fish, that is. Then, amazingly, they were called out of being what they were and taken in a completely different direction. A lot of the people that I meet, Christians and non-Christians, find it very difficult to believe that they really can be called by Jesus out of the limitations and the habits and the shapes of behaviour that have grown and combined over the years to make them what they are.

Looking back into my own life for examples of this, I found myself recalling childhood events that were like templates cut into my life, patterns that threatened to be repeated endlessly as the years went by. One memory that rather surprised me when it surfaced was established during a trip to Austria when I was twelve, a trip whose origins lay, rather bizarrely, in one fleeting moment when I was deeply worried that I might be a direct descendant of Adolf Hitler.

I think I had better explain that.

I was born a few years after the war had ended. Naturally, in the course of my growing-up, there was much relieved and animated talk among family and friends about the mad dictator and the way in which his power-crazed attempts to take over the world had been foiled by the allies. This was exciting and unthreatening, the war being well and truly over, but in a separate, unrelated conversation I overheard my father casually mention that his grandfather had been an Austrian house painter. With a small boy's disregard for clear and contradictory issues of time and space, I felt my blood run cold. The German dictator had been an Austrian house painter. Could I be Adolf Hitler's great-grandson!

Learning through frantically urgent enquiries that I was mistaken in this appalling assumption was like a cold shower on a blazing hot day, despite the laughter that seemed to continue for ever. Such relief! But a heavy residue of interest remained. My ancestral roots were in the soil of a far-off country. At the age of twelve I begged my parents to let me go on a school trip to Austria.

I went.

Guidelines sent out to parents by the school suggested that each boy would need no more than five pounds pocket money for the whole trip. My mother and father were not well off, and five pounds was quite a lot of money in those days, so that was exactly the amount I took. Five pounds! It seemed a fortune to me. I had never owned so much in my life. I was amazed to discover that some other boys had brought ten, fifteen, or even twenty pounds.

I managed my money very badly. By the second day I had spent every penny of my five pounds on sweets and drinks and a gift for my mother. I didn't tell anyone that my supply of pocket money had run out. Salzburg and Innsbruck and all the mountains and the lakes were lovely to look at, but I grew very weary of pretending that I didn't want anything when the others went into shops. I felt like a non-reader forced to spend time with scholars in a library. It was a subtle but profound experience of not belonging.

A couple of days before the end of our holiday the teacher in charge called the group together for a "special" talk. He announced that he had a decision to make, and that we must all be involved in that decision. We formed an intrigued circle in the sitting room of the youth hostel.

"It's about Paul," he said, tilting his head towards the boy sitting rather self-consciously beside him. "Paul tells me he's run out of pocket money. Well, there are still two days to go, so here's my suggestion. I've got some extra money left from what your parents paid. Should we give Paul a little bit of that to keep him going for the rest of the holiday? It's your money really, so it's up to you."

Boys of that age can be gooily sentimental at times. Solemn headshakes, murmurs of approval, and smiles of reassurance for good old Paul were very much the order of the day. This happened a long time ago, but I know for sure that, like Timothy Winters in Charles Causley's poem, no one would have nodded more solemnly, murmured more approvingly, or smiled more reassuringly than the twelve-year-old Adrian Plass. Of course, poor, stony-broke Paul must have a hand-out from the common fund. It was only right. I truly believed that.

The other thing I know for sure is that it never occurred to me for one second that I was in the same sinking financial boat as Paul, nor that I was just as entitled to a helping hand as he was. He had probably run out of money the day before. I had been penniless for days. Strangely, it was not until years later that I was suddenly struck by these undeniable facts. It was as though I regarded the feelings and experiences and ideas of my inner life as a sort of fiction, whereas the concerns of others were non-fiction, touching on, engaging with, and being affected by the real world.

The general principles of that early experience were repeated in various forms again and again until I reached my late thirties. One day, that cave-bound inner life was coaxed and called out into the open air by, I believe, the same person who called these four fishermen.

Having emerged, it took a deep breath and decided to stay. I became a writer, and, in a way, I have been allowed to do my own bit of fishing, for which I sincerely thank God.

If he does call you, do find out what he wants from you. It will change your life.

• ◆ •

Never Mind the Reversing Ducks

WHEN I WAS
A SMALL BOY

On the same sort of subject . . . "When I Was a Small Boy" is a record of my own rather pessimistic fear that the wounds of childhood can never really be healed. The poem is now largely out of date, thank God.

When I was a small boy in a small school,
With endless legs
And ears that widely proclaimed a head full of emergencies,
When I clung by bleeding fingertips
To thirty-three plus nine,
And cognitive dissonance was just a hard sum,
There were only two crimes.
The first was shouting in the corridors,
The second was to be a fool,
And when the bell,
The blessed bell,
Let me fling my body home,
I thought I might, at least, one day, aspire to rule in hell,
But now, I never hear the bell,
And part of me
Will always be
A fool
Screaming, in some sacred corridor.

Clearing Away the Rubbish

PATTERNS FROM
THE PAST

More templates...

In the morning, while it was still very dark, he got up and went out to a deserted place, and there he prayed. And Simon and his companions hunted for him.

When they found him, they said to him, "Everyone is searching for you."

He answered, "Let us go on to the neighboring towns, so that I may proclaim the message there also; for that is what I came out to do."

And he went throughout Galilee, proclaiming the message in their synagogues and casting out demons.

Mark 1 : 35 – 39 NRSV

One thing strikes me immediately about this passage. Jesus doesn't seem to have changed much since he was a boy, does he? His disappearance in the dark, chilly morning and the way in which Simon and the others had to hunt for him, carry echoes of that other time, many years earlier, when the twelve-year-old Jesus did the same thing to his parents. He just slipped away and disappeared. That's what he did then, and that's what he was doing now. In fact, as I spend a moment thinking through the gospel accounts, I become aware that he did quite a lot of disappearing, usually to think and pray, as far as one can tell, occasionally to rest or grieve. It was a pattern in his life and, presumably, an essential one.

So what was happening on this particular morning? They say it is idle to speculate but it's fun to be idle sometimes. Let us speculate.

Jesus wakes in the early hours of the morning after a very short sleep. Perhaps he lies awake for some time, thinking through the events of the previous day. The whole of the important city of Capernaum had been at his door. The *whole* city! Many healings and a lot of deliverance. So many people. Hoards of other desperate folk were bound to turn up throughout the next day as news of the miracles spread. In the face of such overwhelming need, surely it would make sense to simply continue his ministry in the same place on the following day.

And yet . . .

There is a whisper in his ear, a voice reminding him that the obvious thing is not always the right thing, and the wrong thing is helpful neither to God nor to man. So, should he stay or should he go?

The answer to that question was to be found in only one place. Silently, moving with great care so as to wake nobody else, he rises and, wrapping his cloak around his shoulders, slips out into the open air. In a solitary place, somewhere where there will be no distractions, he seeks his Father's will and assurance. By the time the bewildered disciples locate him, long after the sun has crept over the rocky horizon, the decision is made.

Time for a tour of the provinces, and – puzzling for the disciples, no doubt – at a time when the West End run was going so well. The crowds were calling for more and more, and perhaps Jesus was tempted to give them what they wanted. Ultimately, though, he never allowed himself to be motivated by applause nor popularity nor even blatant need. He only did what he saw his Father doing. He knew why he was here, and that pre-dawn rendezvous had clarified and confirmed his spiritual instincts. It was time to go.

Elsewhere I have said that some childhood experiences are like templates cut into our lives, causing negative patterns to be repeated, and this pattern of disappearance in Jesus' life has got me thinking about the template business all over again. I'm not surprised. Reading about Jesus often stirs things up.

I grew up in a house at the bottom of one of the posher streets in our village. Many of the people who lived in Longmeads (the name of our road) were very self-consciously aware that they did *not* live in a scrubby council estate at the other end of the village. Every house in our road was privately owned, and every garden was manicured in that nervously defensive, fussily middle-class way that is particularly English.

In the house next to ours lived Mr and Mrs Jones. He was a teacher and she was a housewife. She was nice and friendly. He was not. In what way not? Well, I had two brothers, one older and one younger. We played constantly in the garden. We played football and cricket and French cricket and a sort of shrunken version of tennis, and we sometimes played an exciting game that involved throwing a tennis ball right over the house so that the person on the other side waited for it to fall out of the sky and tried to catch it. We played in the back garden and we played in the front. Naturally, balls of various shapes and sizes were required for these activities.

From the very beginning Mr Jones *never* let us have our ball back when it crossed the fence into his garden.

We certainly didn't intend our precious footballs or tennis balls to trespass in his sacred domain. Indeed, every time we began another game we assured each other that under no circumstances would such an inconvenient thing be allowed to happen. It did, of course. Small boys may promise themselves and each other the world, but once the game gets going such considerations tend to evaporate. It made Mr Jones very cross. He *would not* give anything back. We could only retrieve our ball by sneaking over the fence when he wasn't looking. My flesh crawls as I recollect undertaking these desperate commando exercises when it was my turn because I was the one who had "done it".

In the house connected to ours on the other side lived Sheila Bourne, a lady who bore a striking resemblance to Queen Elizabeth II. Mrs Bourne was a nurse, and seemed, on the rare occasions when we encountered her, to be very nice, if a little stern. The trouble was that she was a *night* nurse. She worked during the night and slept during the day. Aware as my mother must have been that there was nothing intrinsically wrong with little boys making noise in the course of their play, she constantly worried that our whooping and yelling would wake Sheila, who had apparently complained once or twice that she had been unable to sleep because of our raised voices.

"Sheila's asleep! Play quietly! You'll have to come in if you can't keep the noise down."

During the long holidays my poor mother got quite neurotic about it and, of course, passed a share of her tension to us. Imagine us three boys battling to keep our ball from flying over the hedge on one side and, at the same time, doing our inadequate best to play a hissed, whispering game of football or cricket?

Talk about templates!

Moving into our present house has allowed these memories to surface. For the first time we are in a detached house with no neighbours at all on one side and nothing but fields and distant horizon at the back. We can play music as loudly as we want without worrying about how it affects others. To the small boy in me it feels like a crime – but it's not. Then, soon after we moved in, two anxious-looking little boys from the house next to us appeared on our front step to nervously enquire if they might get their ball back from our garden.

The old choice – revenge or healing?

"Yes," I said, "you can get your ball, and I don't care how many times it comes into our garden. You can always fetch it without having to ask. Even if it comes over a *million* times you can still come and get it back."

Slightly puzzled but beaming with pleasure, they went to collect their ball.

"Never let your play impinge on others, and keep your voice down in case someone's trying to sleep."

There were many positive patterns formed in my early life, but I am surprised to find, on reflection, the extent to which this particular template has negatively affected my friendships, my marriage, my confidence, and my faith. However, a process of healing has been going on for a long time, and God wastes nothing. Give God your dark side. He will rig a few lamps up and use it for something.

— ◆ —

Never Mind the Reversing Ducks

KATY'S
AMAZING THUMB

This selection from *View From a Bouncy Castle* is about my daughter, Kate, someone whose name crops up frequently in my writings, and it illustrates the fact that a simple mistake might produce long-term results that are simply – well, absurd. The family of the church is all too ready to default to safe, ultimately meaningless patterns of behaviour.

The best Easter present I ever had was my daughter Katy. Something brand new had come into my life. I was one of three brothers, one of them two years older than me, the other two years younger. I knew nothing about little girls and how they grow up. It was enormously exciting to have this little jewel of a person living in the same house as me, sharing my life and teaching me so much. As Katy's personality developed so did the things that she said and did. Some of them suggested all sorts of other ideas and connections.

One day, when Katy was still very much a baby, we took a train to Brighton. As the train approached a tunnel just after leaving Lewes Station she put her thumb into her mouth. Our carriage happened to hit the darkness at exactly the same moment. By the light of the sixty-watt bulbs that dully illuminated our carriage Katy removed her thumb from her mouth and stared at it in amazement.

"Good heavens!" she was obviously thinking, "all I have to do is stick this in my mouth and the daylight gets switched off!"

The train emerged from the tunnel and, full of expectancy, she popped her thumb in again. Nothing happened of course, but she was undismayed. All the way down to Brighton, and all the way back later on, she repeated the experiment with little loss of enthusiasm.

I couldn't help reflecting that many denominations are founded on less. . . .

View From a Bouncy Castle

TEA OR COFFEE

Don't get too pessimistic. The most strongly established patterns can be broken or changed when you least expect it. Here's a true story as found in *When You Walk*, which offers proof of that assertion.

An article I read a while ago claimed that radical change is more or less impossible for individuals. Depressing, eh? But – good news! I *know* it's not true.

For years my son Matthew was a tea fanatic. He regularly pointed out that Bridget and I had totally misunderstood the successful preparation of this wonderful beverage. We became jitteringly nervous about preparing tea for him in case it fell short of his high standards – he being a sort of High Priest of the tea-worshipping fraternity.

The rest of the fraternity, Matthew's friends, that is, were just as single-minded. They regarded the very existence of coffee (which we loved, but consumed in dark corners where our shameful apostasy was hidden) as a shocking heresy. They gathered like some loony sect in our kitchen, fussing and fiddling and muttering over their boiling and brewing and sugaring before bearing the sacred vessels on the sacred tray aloft to the High Priest's chaotic Holy of Holies upstairs. Sadly, the ensuing ceremony rarely concluded with ritual returning and cleansing of the sacred vessels. We sad, coffee-drinking acolytes fulfilled that humble role.

Matthew's obsession with tea was unabated as he left for University. It was a fixed point in our universe. It *was* reality.

Then, arriving home during his third year, Matthew lightly declared, "Think I'll have a nice cup of coffee."

"B-b-b-but, Matthew," stammered Bridget, "you don't drink coffee. You *hate* coffee! You drink tea."

Matthew stared at his mother as if she was mad, then, as he explored the long tunnel of his past, seeking some basis for what she'd said, his face cleared.

"Ah, well, yes, I used to have the odd cup of tea, but I always drink coffee now – can't stand *tea*. It's so insipid, don't you think?"

Silly, isn't it, but Matthew's switch from tea to coffee amazed me as much as anything I've ever seen. And to those of us who really want to change but have become resigned to the fact that we probably never will, it gives at least a little hope.

◆

Adapted from *When You Walk*

THE SIX-FORTY
TO CHARING CROSS

Sometimes it requires an act of simple, perhaps painful obedience to break into a repetitive set of events that is bringing us to the brink of disaster.

Jesus once said: "If your right eye causes you to sin, pull it out and throw it away. And if your right hand causes you to sin, cut it off and throw it away."

"It's better," he said, "for an eye and a hand to be lost than for your whole body to end up in hell."

Knowing what a lust human beings exhibit for the formation of new denominations and sects, it amazes me that we have not seen the development of groups of people whose members literally lop pieces off themselves and each other.

When I was going through my own very literal phase, the rather drastic approach to combating sin that these verses suggested was very alarming, especially when I considered my own personal failings. If I had decided to remove the parts of me that caused most problems I would have ended up a decapitated eunuch – at least!

If, however, we agree and accept that Jesus did not intend us to interpret his words literally, what did he mean? I'm sure there are many shades of explanation, all quite valid. How about this one?

A friend of mine, whom I shall call Veronica, worked in a London office each week from Monday to Friday. Every morning she drove to the little country railway station near her home in time to catch the six-forty to Charing Cross. She didn't have to catch that particular train. The one that left at seven o'clock would have done just as well, but Veronica was one of those people who like to arrive early at their place of work, so that there's time to relax and take stock before launching into the business of the day.

The salary that Veronica earned was just what she and her husband Derek needed to keep their joint income at a reasonable level (Derek was a self-employed sculptor who worked from home). They were a very happily married couple in their mid-thirties, an excellent advertisement for commitment.

The months passed and in the course of her regular commuting, Veronica developed a nodding acquaintance with a fellow traveller – a man – who invariably boarded the same train as she did, but at the next station along the line.

Gradually, almost imperceptibly, a friendship began and was deepened each morning during the hour-long trip to London. The man who sat on the opposite seat every day was civilised and charming, a very attractive person. Veronica was forced to face the fact that she had become that very rare creature, a happy commuter. Her heart beat a little faster each time she boarded the train and found herself facing her new friend once again. She was on the verge of falling in love.

This is not, of course, a rare phenomenon in married people, and in many other cases might well have been an indication of neglect or thoughtlessness on the part of the husband, but Veronica and Derek really were very close and valued their relationship highly.

Veronica was troubled and unsure what to do. After much thought she decided to ask for advice from her best friend – her husband. On the Saturday morning following that decision, she sat Derek down with a whisky and soda in the living-room and told him exactly what she was feeling.

Honesty compels me to admit that if I had been in Derek's position that morning I would almost certainly have produced some kind of ragged emotional response. I used to tell myself that I was the civilised level-headed type who could handle any crisis with deep, dark-brown-voiced calm. Experience has shown, however, that a small, high-pitched hysteric usually takes over on these occasions.

Not so in Derek's case. He is a pipe smoking, philosophical chap, the sort of man who enjoys pondering contentedly over a pint. He listened carefully to everything that Veronica said, sipping his drink occasionally and nodding in an understanding sort of way. Finally she ran out of words and sat anxiously on the sofa waiting to hear what her husband would say.

There was a long pause, then Veronica spoke once more.

"I don't know what to do, Derek – tell me what to do."

Slowly and deliberately he rose to his feet, crossed to the sofa and sat down beside his wife. Placing his arm around her shoulders he spoke gently but firmly:

"Darling – change trains."

If the six-forty to Charing Cross causes you to sin (don't cut it off exactly, British Rail will probably do that for you), go on the seven o'clock. Change trains.

Now, even I'm not naïve enough to believe that all or even most problems of this kind can be solved so simply. Even in Veronica's case, it cost her quite a lot to abandon the growing relationship that had brightened her mornings. It was worth it for her. For others there will be such complex considerations and so many difficulties, or perhaps things have gone so far, that the "changing trains" option is just not feasible.

But for people, Christian or otherwise, who want to avoid problems in the future, it is worth considering the proposition that it is easier to steer our lives and temperaments round obstacles rather than meet them head-on, wrestle desperately with them, and probably lose the contest. Most of us know only too well the areas in which we are weak or likely to be tempted. Often it takes a lot of courage and determination to change direction when sweet darkness is only a step away.

I know that Veronica's story doesn't sound very much like the Bible verses that I quoted, but it comes down to the same thing in the end, and the general principle holds good in all sorts of different situations. If you run into trouble, and it's not too late to do something about it, don't mess about – change trains.

View From a Bouncy Castle

PRAISE OFFERED
AS SACRIFICE

I've discovered (the hard way) that you can't give your spiritual life a boost by simply inserting some new set of behaviours into your personality as though you were putting a new programme on the computer. God deals with real people in real ways, and the sooner we accept that the better. In the following piece that is exactly the lesson that the diarist has to learn after getting very fed-up with his family.

Friday 4 March

Odd day today. Started badly and ended well.

The bad start was when I woke up determined to put into practise something I read in a magazine article last night about "Praise Offered as Sacrifice". The writer of the article said that we should be especially willing to give praise and worship to God at times when we don't feel like doing it. If we made this sacrifice, the article explained, God would reward us by turning our act of will into a veritable hymn of spontaneous joy that would bless us and all those around us.

Started as soon as I woke, feeling, as usual, like a dead slug, by saying "Praise the Lord!" four or five times as I lay staring at the ceiling. Felt a bit strange and I sounded a bit croaky, but the article did say that one had to persist until one came through into the place of transfiguration. Occurred to me that if I got through a lot of praise very quickly the speed of "coming through" might be concertinaed, as it were.

Said, "Praise the Lord! Hallelujah! Amen!" very rapidly and repeatedly as I got out of bed and put my dressing gown on. Caught a glimpse of Anne's face peering over the bedclothes as I went out of the room. Her eyes were wild and staring. Continued praising by an act of the will all the way along the landing and into the bathroom. Carried on all through my shower and while I was in the lavatory. Flagging a bit by the time I made the return trip along the landing, but still managed to emit the odd "Praise the Lord".

No sign at breakfast that my act of will had been transformed into a hymn of joy that would bless me and all those around me. On the contrary – those around me (Anne and Gerald) looked more morose and unhappy and unblessed than usual.

Asked what was wrong.

Anne rubbed her eyes and said wearily, "Adrian, I don't know what harebrained scheme you're pursuing at the moment, and, to be honest, I don't really care. What I do care about is the way it affects me. I want to make it very clear that I don't appreciate being woken – early – out of what *was* a beautiful sleep by a religious maniac who is incapable of keeping his wretched outpourings to himself."

"Wretched outpourings? I can't believe you're calling – "

"It really does puzzle me that, after all these years, and knowing what you know about the sheer – the sheer *sanity* of God, that you go on being sucked in by these half-baked twits who can't relax until they've got other people behaving in the same bizarre fashion as themselves."

"I'll have you know," I said with dignity, "that this particular 'half-baked twit', as you so uncharitably call him, has one of the most respected ministries in this country. More than twenty fellowships come under his umbrella."

Anne said, "Well, I hope the weather keeps fine for them."

"That's not funny," I said.

"Yes, it is!" cackled Gerald.

Really made me cross. "And what about you, Gerald – have you got something serious to say about this morning? Or are you just going to make a joke of it as usual?"

Gerald shrugged. "Well, I didn't have to suffer the awful awakening that Mum did, but I heard just about everything else after that. It was pretty awful, Dad. It sounded as though a Pentecostal convention was being held in our bathroom with a fringe praise-meeting going on in the loo. Then I heard you still muttering stuff along the landing on your way back to your room. It *was* a bit wearing."

"I see. A bit wearing. And presumably you would agree with your mother's restrained description of my sacrifice of praise as the 'wretched outpourings of a religious maniac', would you?"

"Oh, no," said Gerald, "I don't think I'd describe it like that. No – when I was listening to you in the bathroom and the toilet this morning it reminded me of something else, but I couldn't quite put my finger on what it was." He paused and thought for a moment. "Ah, yes, that's it! I know what it was. I think I'd describe it as a sort of – spiritual flatulence. Morning was breaking."

Too angry to speak. Went up and shut myself in my study until they'd both gone out. Hoped that as the day went by they'd start to feel guilty and ashamed about the way they'd spoken to me. I planned to be hurt and not easily consoled, but eventually forgive them.

Had to leave for my evening speaking engagement before Anne and Gerald came home. Richard Cook had offered to drive me in our car so that I'd be fresh for the meeting when I got there. Set off about half past four.

Sometimes wish Richard's sense of humour was just a little more highly developed. We turned into a nearby garage to get some petrol, and just as we were approaching the pumps, Richard said, "Is the petrol cap on your side?"

I said, "Well, it's always been very supportive."

He said, "No, I mean – which side of the car is the petrol cap?"

Richard dropped me off at Wopsley Community Fellowship Church at about six-thirty before driving away to visit an aunt who lived locally.

First time I'd ever been to this church. Felt a bit lonely and isolated, especially after what had happened with Anne and Gerald in the morning. Had a bad attack of the "What-on-earth-is-a-person-like-me-doing-here?" jitters. What would these trusting people say if they knew that their guest speaker was still in the middle of a giant sulk with his wife and son? Wished Anne and Gerald were there so that we could all say sorry and hug each other and make everything all right.

Talk went all right, I suppose, then afterwards coffee and cakes were served so that people could "chat" while they circulated. Must say it was a very warm, friendly, relaxed atmosphere. Looked around the church for the first time (I never notice anything until after I've spoken) and saw that it was very plain except for a large, highly complex but very crudely carved wooden cross on the wall above the shallow stage at the front. Commented on it to an elderly lady carrying a tray of coffee around.

She said cheerfully, "Ah, yes, that's our cross. We don't like that at all."

She moved on with her tray before I could ask her what she meant.

Pointed out the cross a little later to a youngish man who was busy stacking chairs to make room for people to "circulate".

I said, "That's a fine cross you have up there."

He stopped for a moment, wiped his forehead, and looked quite surprised. "Do you really like it? We think it's hideous. Just the place for it, though, up in front there, don't you think?"

"Yes, but why – "

He'd gone.

Finally nobbled Daniel Bisset, the elder-in-charge, a large, happy man, who seemed to be everybody's friend, and asked him about the cross.

"Ah, yes!" Daniel nodded and beamed. "We're very proud of that ugly old cross, we really are. You see, we always said we'd never have such things here. Had a special meeting, we did, eleven or twelve years ago when we got started, and the whole caboodle of us agreed that we didn't want any such stuff cluttering up the place. That's why it's so good to see it up there now – makes it even more important, if you see what I mean."

I said, "No, I'm sorry, I don't see what you mean at all. Everyone I talk to about that cross tells me how much you don't want it here, and in the same breath they tell me how proud you all are of it. I don't understand at all."

Daniel guffawed loudly. "See what you mean, see what you mean – okay, I'll tell you what happened. It's all about this old chap called Eric Carter – lived on his own up in one of those slummy cottages that used to be where the back of Sainsbury's is now. Eric was in his – ooh, his mid-seventies when I first met him, couldn't see too well, and he was a real old pagan, according to his own estimate. We met him when some of the harvest stuff got taken round his house one Monday after the service, and whoever it was went round left a list of things going on at the church. Well, Eric was a wary old devil, and a bit crabby at first, but he was lonely, so he did turn up at one of our social evenings that we do, and he seemed to have a good time. After that – I dunno, one thing led to another – I saw him round at his home quite a bit as well as him coming to the odd service, and the long and the short of it is that, in the end, he became a Christian. Knelt down like a baby one evening up there at the front and said he wanted to give his life to Jesus."

"And the cross?"

"One day, when I was round visiting him, Eric suddenly says, 'Would it be all right if I said a word or two at the front next Sunday, and can someone pick me up and bring me down?' Well, I was a bit surprised at this because Eric always prided himself on making his own way down to the church whenever he came, but there was no way he was going to tell me what he was on about, so I just agreed to do what he'd asked and that was that.

"The next Sunday, Eric arrives at the church – can't remember who picked him up – and he actually walked into the building pushing the wheelbarrow that we keep in the shed round the back. And lying across the top of this wheelbarrow, not in it because it was too big, was this mystery object wrapped up in sacks and whatnot. Well, you can imagine, by the time Eric got up to do his turn everyone was agog. What *was* he going to say, and what was that *thing* in the wheelbarrow standing next to him? And then old Eric started to say his piece. . . ."

Daniel paused for a moment, his eyes bright with the memory.

"Eric talked about how lonely he'd been before he started coming down to church do's, as he called them, and how surprised he'd been at the friendliness, not just towards him, but among the rest of us. He said how he'd been taught as a kid that you keep yourself to yourself in church so as not to interfere with anyone else, and he'd been afraid it was going to be like that. I can still remember what he said.

"'You all seemed to be lookin' after each other,' those were his words, 'an' makin' sure each other was 'appy. It made me want to be in it. An' now I am. I didn't know it was Jesus doin' it, but I do now.'

"And then he got a bit pink and said he'd made something for the church to thank us for being nice to each other and to him, so that he ended up meeting Jesus. He got one of the lads to come and help him unwrap the thing on the wheelbarrow and hold it up, and, of course, it was that cross that's up the front there now. It would be a sort of sign, he said, of how friendly Jesus wants us to be. Turned out he'd worked on it for weeks in the little shed at the back of his cottage, but, what with poor lighting and him having not very good eyesight anyway, the thing was all over the place, and some of it a very strange shape, as you can see."

"But you put it up."

"'Course we did! That cross comes down over my dead body. It tells us and anyone else who bothers to find out that a man came to Jesus because we were nice to each other. We don't like crosses, but we like *that* cross."

I glanced around. "Is Eric here tonight?"

"Probably," said Daniel with sudden gentleness, "but you won't see him if he is. He died about four years ago – gone to put in a good word for us I hope."

Richard arrived soon after that to take me home. Said he'd had a time of splitting and stacking at his aunt's house. Thought he was talking about some obscure area of dialectical religious philosophy until he explained that he'd been chopping firewood for her.

Both sat in silence for some time on the way back. Then Richard suddenly said, "Ha! Always been very supportive – ha!"

Better late than never, I suppose.

Looking forward all the way home to telling Anne about my conversation with Daniel Bisset. Remembered, just as I walked into the kitchen where Anne and Gerald were sitting over coffee, that I was still in the middle of sulking and being deeply hurt about the reaction to my sacrifice of praise. Had about two seconds to decide whether to be nice or not. . . .

I wonder if Eric Carter knows that his ugly old cross was still doing its work in our kitchen four years after he'd gone?

Anne and I were away until Sunday night for a supposed-to-be-romantic-but-usually-begins-with-a-big-row-and-then-gets-a-lot-better-after-that-if-not-actually-romantic weekend. Anne says if I record a single word of it in here she's going to write a book about what happened on our wedding night.

● ◆ ●

Sacred Diary of Adrian Plass, Christian Speaker,
Aged Forty-Five and Three Quarters

SMALL
WORLD

"Small World" is one of the short stories from a collection called *Nothing but the Truth*. It describes the path to a sudden and unexpected revelation after the establishment and tragic disruption of a pattern of encounters between father and son.

They say you should never go back.

I read a short story once that began with those exact words, and broadly speaking I suppose at the time when I read them I would have agreed. You never know what's going to happen when you take the risk of going back. That's why I was so surprised to find myself on Platform Nine of Clapham Junction Railway Station at a quarter to ten one cold autumn morning, probably the coldest of the year so far, waiting for a train that would take me to Winchester for the first time for more than two decades.

With less than ten minutes to go before the train was due to arrive, part of me didn't really believe I would actually get on when it rumbled to a halt. Why in a month of Sundays, I kept asking myself, should I actively court the pain and disappointment that could easily result from such an emotionally loaded expedition? What was the point of risking some kind of inner disaster when, at a pinch, I could manage to go on living with the tightly tied knot that had been in my stomach since I was a young boy? It was my wife who had finally persuaded me to do the thing I feared so much.

"You may be able to go on living with it," she said one day, "but I'm not sure the rest of us can. Seriously, John, why don't you pick a day and just go. I know it won't be easy, but you'll be so glad when you've done it. I'll come with you if you want. I tell you what – I'll take you out and buy you an Indian meal as a reward when you get back."

She was deliberately being flippant about something that really mattered to her, but she was right. There's something about the idea of an Indian meal that brightens just about anything up. It was the trigger. I said I'd go, but on my own.

"Winchester, Winchester, Winchester . . ." I whispered the word neurotically over and over to myself as I paced up and down the long platform trying to keep warm. For me, the very word sagged with significance, like one of those poems that tries to make you feel too much.

I did board the 9.56 when it arrived. If I hadn't been as frozen as I was I might have dithered and changed my mind, but it was *so* wonderful to step into the heated interior of the train. Not only that, but I also found a vacant window seat by a table almost immediately.

On the other side of the table sat a young chap of about eighteen, lost in the private world of his personal stereo. Outside this little universe all that could be heard of the recorded sound was a featureless buzz. Settling back into the warmth and comfort of my new surroundings I found myself idly wondering if this was a happy person. He looked quite together and content I thought, the sort of young man who is just beginning to feel a genuine confidence in himself. He had a well-cared-for, secure look about him. Good parents probably. A mother who'd consistently done her very best for him, a father who was never intrusive but always there if he was needed when things started to fall apart. Sports. Advice. All that stuff. Yes, by the look of him that was exactly the sort of father he'd got. And would he realise just how bloody fortunate he was in that respect? Oh, no! You could bet your life he . . .

I squirmed in my seat as all the old boringly familiar feelings of helpless rage began to mount in me. How long was I going to have to put up with the past reaching out to grab me by the throat like this? What a maniac I was becoming. Pushing the hair brusquely back from my forehead with one hand, I dragged my attention away from the innocent music lover on the other side of the table and gazed out of the window. As if in some fever dream, I rehearsed the past in my mind as I had done a thousand times, helplessly aware that ten thousand repetitions would never make any difference to the way things had been.

I never had fully understood why my parents separated. I lived with my mother, a very efficient, undemonstrative, quietly unhappy woman. The only thing she ever said about the failure of her marriage was in answer to an unusually direct question when I was about ten.

"Why did Daddy go away and leave us when I was little?"

"Your father can only cope with very small worlds."

That was all she said and all she would say. It was typically enigmatic. What was a ten-year-old supposed to do with that? I hadn't the faintest idea what she was talking about. Perhaps if I'd thought about it a little more I might have begun to understand. After all, Dad had created a little world for him and me to be together in, and it hardly changed at all in the short time that I knew him.

It began a few days after my eighth birthday. Mother announced quite dispassionately one morning that my father had come back to England to live. He wanted to see me that afternoon in Winchester. Did I want to go?

I knew I had a dad, but he'd left when I was little more than a baby, so I had no memory of him at all. My mother kept no photographs of her ex-husband in our house. Many times, in the course of my early years, I had lain awake at night, picturing his face just above the end of the bed in the darkness of my room, and imagined making a special trip to find him. In my fantasies he was always overjoyed to see me. We would embrace, and he would explain why it had been so difficult for us to be together and say how much he had missed me since going away.

Here was a chance to see him in reality. I felt shy but excited. I remembered looking into my mother's face, searching for a clue to the solution of the obvious problem. Did she want me to go? But my mother's face never gave information of that sort. There were no clues.

"Yes, please," I said, "I'd like to go, mother."

Later that morning my mother drove me to Winchester in our blue mini. We stopped just outside the Old Market Inn. There was a man leaning against a gatepost a few yards away. Mother didn't even get out. So much for my secretly cherished dreams of parental reunion!

"That's your father," she said, pointing. "You'll like him. I'll pick you up again at five o'clock."

Suddenly, there I was, at eight years of age, standing outside a pub in a strange city with a strange man, watching the familiar shape of our little car accelerate away and disappear round the corner. Looking back, I can hardly believe what my mother did. I cannot begin to imagine doing anything so clearly irresponsible with one of my own children. For a few seconds I did experience real panic, but small children readily accept bizarre things, and, in any case, my mother had told me I would like my father, and she was the sort of woman for whom every opinion laid down was a winning card. I had never known her to be wrong before.

Nor was she wrong now. All he said in a quiet, resonant voice as I walked hesitantly in his direction, was, "John? I'm your dad," but his eyes smiled from far inside, and there was a feeling of safeness about him. I recall being obscurely pleased that he continued to lean on the gatepost as I moved towards him. He let me do the last bit of the trip.

This first meeting was a long way from the emotional splurge of my night-time fantasies, but from the moment I encountered my father's chuckling good humour I absolutely adored him. That day we sat on the grass outside the cathedral in the sunshine and ate our way through a picnic he'd brought. I remember every crumb. There were three different kinds of sandwich – ham, banana, and cheese – two kinds of cake – Battenburg and cherry – two chocolate biscuits wrapped in shiny coloured paper, and an apple each. There was a bottle filled with ready-diluted lemon squash and two disposable paper cups to drink it from.

He asked me questions about myself as we ate, listening in a very still way with his head on one side as I gained confidence and chattered away about home and school and friends and football.

When he asked me which team I supported I suspended the whole of my beloved Arsenal team and said, "Which one do you support?"

"Aston Villa," he replied.

"So do I," I said, and from that day forward I did.

When we'd finished eating he packed everything away in a brown and green leather shopping bag and stood up.

"Well, John," he smiled, "do you think we're going to be pals?"

I looked at him then and thought to myself that he was a "hands in his pockets" sort of man. His clothes were brown and soft, so were his face and hair. He was comfortably untidy and his eyes seemed a little bit hurt as well as being smiley and kind.

"Oh, yes, Dad," I said, relishing this word that had suddenly become so unexpectedly and wonderfully substantial, "we'll be pals all right."

We spent the rest of the afternoon walking slowly round the inside of the cathedral, stopping every now and then for me to ask a question, or when Dad wanted to explain something. He seemed to know an awful lot about everything without having to use a guide, and I think I sensed, even then, that he was introducing me to something he loved.

Mother picked me up at five o'clock – on the dot, of course. She didn't get out of the car this time either or even look in the direction of my father, as far as I could see. Poor Mother. I'm sure I must have rabbited on about my new "pal" all the way back home, but all I can remember her saying was, "I told you you'd like him".

"But," I said in real puzzlement to myself in bed that night, "how could you possibly *not* like someone so nice?"

Three or four times a year for the next four years the pattern of that first visit was repeated. There might be fruit cake instead of Battenburg, and the weather might drive us under cover to eat our picnic sometimes, but in every other way our outings stayed exactly the same, from the brown and green leather shopping bag to the paper cups. It never struck me as odd that we always met in the same way, and always did the same things. On the contrary, I loved it. I loved him. It was simply the way things were. I didn't mind in the least that I never saw where he lived and never really learned anything about the rest of his life, because we seemed to belong to each other totally for as long as those all too infrequent afternoons lasted, and that was all that mattered to me. As time went by Winchester Cathedral and everything connected with it glowed richly in my imagination with a sparkling Christmassy brightness, a reflection of the joy I found in just being there with my father.

He died at the wrong time, you see. I was twelve. It was two days before my next visit was due. When my mother gave me the news, delivered in that same dry, disinterested way, it was like being punched in the stomach very hard when you're not expecting it. And then – well, I've never been quite sure what happened then. I think I managed to switch something off right inside me, and I felt nothing. I don't know if I was ever quite able to forgive my mother for the way she dealt with me over my father's death. I wasn't taken to any kind of service and there was no grave because his body had been cremated. The ashes were distributed somewhere or other by somebody, my mother said, with an almost non-existent emphasis on the "somebody", and that was it. He was gone. Nothing to remind me of him, and a complete inability to grieve. I don't think I shed a single tear.

The years went by. I grew up. I got married. My mother died. I had two children. I was very nearly happy – happy but for the nagging, ever-present knowledge that one day I was going to have to deal with the little unexploded bomb that lay like a lump of cold metal in the pit of my stomach. I was never quite brave enough to face it, the mixture of grief, sorrow, and heartache that might explode and tear me to pieces. I kept well away from Winchester.

Now my wife had talked me into going back. She had seen, over the years, how the pain of this emotional containment affected not just me but her and the children as well. Often it manifested itself in black moods that had no very clear link to the past but were nevertheless closely connected with those distant days.

Sometimes specific incidents triggered irrational bouts of anger. When Sam, aged nine, asked me why I supported a "rubbish team" like

Aston Villa, I flew into a terrible rage, demanding to know why I shouldn't and what it had got to do with him. For that brief, black period I felt as if I was eight years old and he was bullying me. Realising what was really going on was so strange – like regaining consciousness after a particularly vivid dream. Poor, confused Sam forgave me freely.

Another time, I was walking around the local shopping precinct with my wife, when I happened to notice that a woman walking beside me was carrying a shopping bag that closely resembled the one my father used to pack our picnics in. Brown leather with inlaid green patches. The sight of it made me feel sick in my stomach. I was low for days. So many things . . .

Well, I was going to tackle it now. Soon after alighting from this train I would be stepping back into the only world that my father and I had ever shared. Resting my face against the cold surface of the window I closed my eyes and dozed fitfully for the rest of the hour-long journey.

By 11.15 I was sitting in the warmth and comfort of the Old Market Inn in Winchester. The walk down from the station had set up such a screaming tension in me that my hands and teeth were tightly clenched by the time I turned into Market Street, but I was beginning to feel a little better now. I couldn't have faced going into the cathedral straight away, and the only delaying tactic that I could think of was the pub. I'm not a great drinker at the best of times, let alone on an occasion like this, so I simply ordered a hot chocolate and took it over to a seat by the window that looked out towards the cathedral. Resting my elbows on the table in front of me I cuddled the hot china mug in my hands. It felt like a mini-version of one of those old stone hot water bottles that I could just remember having in bed with me when I stayed with my grandmother as a small child.

Through the window I could see, a hundred yards away, the west door of the cathedral, the door that my dad and I had walked through so many times. Now, on this desolately bleak October afternoon, a mere trickle of warmly dressed visitors was passing in and out of the building.

I decided to give myself a talking to.

"Now look!" I whispered into the side of my mug, "you are an adult. You are not a child. You are allowed to choose what to do for yourself. If you decide to get up and walk back to the station and take the next train home, then that is fine. That is absolutely fine. You've lived with this fear in your gut for twenty years. You might as well put up with it for another decade or two. Why tear yourself to pieces for nothing? Give up! Go home! You don't even really know what you're looking for, and you probably won't find it here anyway. Apart from anything else, how are you going to handle a thumping great anticlimax, if that's what it turns out to be? Go on – go home. Finish your hot drink and get back to the station."

Haranguing myself like this has always helped me to make decisions, and it did now. I stood up, buttoned my overcoat, wrapped my scarf round my neck, and left the pub. Seconds later, breathless with quivering anticipation and the icy cold, I was striding across the Close with almost robotic determination towards the west door. I was about to pay my first visit to Winchester Cathedral since the year of my twelfth birthday. As I reached the door and pushed it open I realised that it was also the only time I had ever entered it on my own.

Despite the cold I was perspiring heavily as I came through the inner door and stood motionless for a moment at the west end of the nave. The abruptly overpowering familiarity of my surroundings made me feel quite faint. Then, suddenly filled with a brittle excitement, I swung round and peered up at the strange jumble of stained-glass fragments that almost filled the top half of the west wall.

"What's that all about then, John?"

I remembered the question. I remembered my answer.

"Cromwell smashed a window, Dad, and the people saved the pieces and hid 'em and tried to put them back together later, but they couldn't get it right so they put them all over the place like a giant jigsaw puzzle so they'd still got their window, whatever old Cromwell thought he'd done. Is that right, Dad?"

It was right. It was right! Dad had told me, so it must be right.

I turned round and started to walk along the south aisle. I was in a trance. I was twelve years old. I remembered everything. There was Doctor Warton's memorial, and there, listening forever to their famous headmaster, were three of his pupils dressed in their funny old-fashioned clothes.

"Where will we find three little tiny monks, John?"

I was *so* proud.

"Over here, Dad, sitting by the bishop's feet."

And then, a bit farther up, the list of people from something called the Hampshire regiment, who had all been killed in the war.

"Listen, Dad! Listen! Listen! Listen to the names – Shadwell, Smallpiece, Smith, Spanner, Stammer, Steele, Stone. Are they real names, Dad?"

"Yes, they're real names and they really did die, son."

On to the South Transept, and the oldest oak chairs in England.

"Are we allowed to sit on them, Dad?"

"Yes, go on. Nothing to say you can't, is there? They've put up with four hundred years of assorted English bottoms. If yours makes much difference it's probably time for them to be turned into firewood anyway."

I always sat on both of them, enthralled by the thought of those hundreds and hundreds of different backsides perching there over the years.

Next came the grave of Isaak Walton, the fisherman, followed by the memorial to Bishop Wilberforce, son of the man who tried to free all the slaves. Over there were the Pilgrim Gates, and up to the left, in their chests on top of the wall, were the bones of the old kings. Most frightening to me as a small boy was the horrible cadaver of Bishop Fox in its tiny prison behind iron bars, put there by him to remind the world that no one lives forever.

Oh, Dad . . .

I came to a place where candles glowed and flickered on a wrought-iron stand. Taking a fresh candle I lit it from one of the others and put a coin in the nearby box. Stepping back, I stared at the little flame as it wavered and nearly died before starting to burn steadily. The candle was for my father. Its flame was alive, and he was dead. I began to perspire again. That bomb inside me was about to go off and I was terrified. Instinctively I moved away from a small group of people who were peering at something beside me and turned quickly into the retro choir, deserted now, but filled, like every other corner of this building, with four years of Dad and me.

"See those words under that grille, son? They're all about St Swithun, the saint of the cathedral. Do you remember what that first bit means?"

"Whatever partakes of God is safe in God. Right, Dad?"

"Right, son."

I couldn't stand it any more. I had to get out. I set off down the north presbytery aisle, intending to head straight for the exit at the other end of the building, but a loud group of tourists forced me aside into the choir, and suddenly I knew, like a child desperate not to throw up in the wrong place, that I wasn't going to make it. I crumpled on to one of the front choir stalls at the foot of the presbytery steps, trying to look as if I was intensely interested in the tomb of Rufus, the Norman king who died mysteriously in the New Forest.

"What did they find when they opened old Rufus up, John?"

"An arrowhead, Dad. Somebody shot him!"

"Oh, Dad, oh, Dad! Why did you die?"

I slumped forward, my face in my hands, and wept. The explosion wasn't as wildly violent as I'd feared, but the sobs that passed through my body in wave after shuddering wave shook everything in me. And there was so much anger in it. Grief I'd expected, but not anger. Perhaps that was why I'd switched off after that first thudding shock all those years ago. Probably I just couldn't handle the idea of expressing intense fury to someone I had loved so much.

I certainly expressed it now.

"You left me! You left me alone! You just left me! Oh, Dad, why did you leave me?"

Sheer strength of feeling drove me to my feet. As far as I can remember there was nobody else in the choir, but I honestly don't think I'd have noticed if there had been. And it was at that moment, through the tears that had waited so long to be shed, that I found my eyes fixed on Dad's favourite thing of all, the carved figure of Christ on the cross right at the centre of the great screen above the high altar.

For one of the very few times in my life, some words of Jesus came, quite unbidden, to my mind.

"My God! My God! Why have you forsaken me?"

Whatever partakes of God is safe in God.

"Is that right, Dad?"

"That's right, son."

A small world.

Nothing but the Truth

Part Four

PRIORITIES

Priorities are tricky, slippery things. Most of us have a good, theoretical understanding of the most important things in life, but when it comes to the crunch – all sorts of crunches – we discover what actually occupies the number one spot on our personal agenda. I have had to learn so many lessons in this area – as you will see.

DAFFODIL

In the year when Katy became three, I strolled into the garden one sparkling April morning, to find my diminutive daughter pushing one arm up as far as it would go towards the sky. In her outstretched hand was a single bluebell, newly picked from the border beside the lawn. As she offered her flower to the shining early sun, she identified it with a loud ecstatic cry.

"DAFFODIL!!" she shouted, "DAFFOD-I-IL!!"

I am as tediously obsessed with accuracy as most parents. I corrected her gently.

"No darling," I said, "it's a bluebell."

Not one inch did she reduce the length of her stretching arm, not one decibel did she lower her volume: "BLUEBELL!!" she shouted, "BLUE-BE-E-ELL!"

Katy's joy was in being part of the morning and having a beautiful flower, not in anything so trivial as being right. She accepted my pedantic correction, but it didn't change anything important.

If only those of us who are Christians were more like Katy in the garden, less concerned with how right we are in our individual emphases and dogmas than with the joy of being one with Jesus.

"YOU HAVE TO SPEAK IN TONGUES TO BE A CHRISTIAN!!" one of us might shout ecstatically.

"No you don't," God might correct us gently.

"YOU DON'T HAVE TO SPEAK IN TONGUES TO BE A CHRISTIAN!!" we would shout with undiminished joy.

View From A Bouncy Castle

WHEN THE
CRUNCH COMES

One of my favourite Old Testament characters, Gideon found that God was about to turn his priorities upside down.

> The angel of the LORD came and sat down under the oak in Ophrah that belonged to Joash the Abiezrite, where his son Gideon was threshing wheat in a winepress to keep it from the Midianites.
>
> When the angel of the LORD appeared to Gideon, he said, "The LORD is with you, mighty warrior."
>
> "But, sir," Gideon replied, "if the LORD is with us, why has all this happened to us? Where are all his wonders that our fathers told us about when they said, 'Did not the LORD bring us up out of Egypt?' But now the LORD has abandoned us and put us into the hands of Midian."
>
> The LORD turned to him and said, "Go in the strength you have and save Israel out of Midian's hand. Am I not sending you?"
>
> "But, LORD," Gideon asked, "how can I save Israel? My clan is the weakest in Manasseh, and I am the least in my family."
>
> The LORD answered, "I will be with you, and you will strike down all the Midianites together."
>
> Judges 6 : 11 – 16

I suppose angels get used to carrying out daft-sounding orders without question. This one must have been amazed when he was told to go and address Gideon, of all people, as "Mighty Warrior". Gideon was singularly unimpressed, wasn't he? So would I have been, if I was the least important member of the least important family in the whole community, and some stranger with an advanced case of religious mania had solemnly announced that I was going to defeat the entire opposing army as if they were one man. I'd have been on the phone to the local psychiatric facility insisting that they check numbers. And even if this was a messenger from the Lord there was little recent evidence to suggest that God had either the power or the inclination to intervene as he had done in the past.

Gideon was going to take a lot of convincing, and I don't blame him. I know how it feels to be inwardly programmed for failure. I have felt small and useless. I've experienced the gnawing fear that when some awful crunch situation comes along I shall betray the people who rely on me most. Sometimes, usually in the middle of the night, I'm gripped by panic as my imagination pumps out grisly scenes in which members of my family die dreadful deaths while I stand uselessly aside, paralysed by fear and inadequacy.

Curiously enough, although these fears are completely genuine, my response on the only occasion when I was tested in this way suggested that they might be quite unfounded. I'm aware that this will seem a very trivial incident, especially to those of my readers who have rescued people from burning buildings and wrestled with man-eating tigers, but it meant a lot to me.

Bridget and I had driven out one morning to a nearby village to visit a traditional tea-room whose beverages and cakes were, in our very humble opinion, the best in Sussex. We were particularly anxious that the trip should be a successful one because our last visit to this wonderful establishment had ended rather abruptly, when baby Katy threw up about as comprehensively as it can be done. The Plass children have always been generous with their undigested stomach contents, and Katy was no exception. She shared hers liberally and without favour between as many of our fellow-customers as she could reach in one, unconsciously artistic, spinning, centrifugal outpouring. The proprietors were very nice about it. They insisted that we should come back soon, but as we removed the husk of our little green daughter from the somewhat depressed, swamp-like atmosphere that she had created, we doubted that we would ever return.

Now, lured by base desire for more of those exceptional cakes, we were back!

This time Katy was not sick, and we rejoiced over our total rehabilitation. We rejoiced a little too much. Or rather, I did. As we headed for the car, full of tea and cake, I did a small skip of celebration with Katy in my arms and suddenly felt my balance slipping irretrievably away. I was about to fall flat on my face with Katy sandwiched between my considerable bulk and the hard tarmac of the car-park. I didn't make any heroic decisions – there was no time for that. Katy not being hurt was all that mattered. Somehow I managed to twist my body in mid-topple, as it were, so that I landed on my back instead of my front. I was winded, and a bit bruised and scraped, but Katy was fine, if a little puzzled by our new game.

In the end it was the relationship that produced the spontaneous response, and, of course, it would have been exactly the same for any parent who loved his child.

I suspect that we would be well advised to concentrate on developing our closeness to Jesus, rather than dwelling gloomily on the probability that we will let him down, because it will be the reality or otherwise of that relationship that makes the difference when the crunch comes.

Pray with Me

Father, it would be very foolish of us to pray for a crunch to come. Who needs unnecessary crunches? We know, though, that if we intend to follow you, anything can happen, and we want to be ready. When the testing time comes, may our love for you be greater than our fear. We would like to be so close to you that we are able to not only say, like Jesus at Gethsemane, "Not my will be done, but yours", but mean it as well.

An awful lot of us are simply not in that place yet. Teach us individually how to strengthen the bond we have with you. We will try to talk more openly and more often with you. We will try to listen more to your voice. We will try to recognise you in the suffering folks around us. We will try to follow you into dark and dangerous places, and after that – it's up to you. Amen.

The Unlocking

I AM A STUDY
GROUP LEADER

The Sacred Diary again, and Adrian has a hard but necessary lesson to learn about putting family first.

Wednesday 9 April

Edwin, our elder, phoned to confirm that it was all right for the study-group to meet here tomorrow night.

Thursday 10 April

Study-group began as usual about eight o'clock. Deliberately sat on the floor near the door, so that I could escape easily if I had to.

Started with a discussion on euthanasia. Deaf old Mrs Thynn shocked everyone by saying that she thought it was absolutely lovely, and she'd like her grandchildren to have a chance to sit and watch it from beginning to end!

Stunned silence until Anne suddenly giggled and said, "She thinks it's a Walt Disney film." General atmosphere of relief, except from Richard Cook, who'd obviously been about to fire several rounds of Scripture from the hip.

Discussion droned on.

Kept my eyes open during the prayer time. Everyone else locked in the "shampoo position", as Gerald calls it. Wondered how many were sincere. Decided not many.

Edwin stayed on afterwards. Said he wanted a "chat". Felt a little nervous. Edwin *knows* things sometimes.

"Cheer up!" said Edwin, "I've got a little job to offer you."

Panic!!! "What err . . . job's that then, Edwin?"

"Well, I think – I'm not absolutely sure, mind – but I *think* the Lord wants you to be a study-group leader."

Started babbling about being bad and useless and not clever enough. Edwin interrupted me.

"It was during your testimony at Easter that the idea first came into my head. I was very impressed with how honest and vulnerable you were. Helped a lot of people, you know."

Started to say something, but he held up his hand to stop me.

"Don't give me an answer now. Think about it. Let me know tomorrow. Ask *Him*."

11.45

Prayed in bed with Anne just now.

She said, "I think Edwin's right."

I like Anne being sure. "Yes," I said, "so do I."

Sat for a while, thinking / worrying / feeling pleased. Suddenly remembered what I'd meant to ask Anne.

"Anne, why did Leonard want to borrow the cat, and – "

She was fast asleep.

1.30 A.M.

Still awake. Hope my group don't go all quiet. Hope George Farmer's one of my group. He'll keep 'em on their toes. . . .

Friday 11 April

Rang Edwin first thing this morning to tell him my decision. Sounded very pleased. Told Gerald at breakfast. He *didn't* make a joke!

I am a study-group leader!

I *am* a study-group leader!!

I am *a* study-group leader!!!

I am a *study-group* leader!!!!

I am a study-group *leader*!!!!!

Thanked God in my quiet-time that I am not a proud man. Can't help feeling a new sense of importance, though. *Me!* A study-group leader! Well, well!

Saturday 12 April

Ridiculous incident this morning, just as I was enjoying my new sensation of deep, spiritual dignity. Busy washing-up and thinking about my first study-group as a leader this Thursday, when I put my hand into the washing-up bowl and cut my thumb quite badly on the bread knife. Started to bleed quite heavily.

Gerald, who was drying-up, said, "How did you do that, Dad?"

"Like this," I said, and put my other hand in the washing-up bowl. Cut my other thumb. Ended up with an absurd, white bulbous bandage on *both* thumbs.

Anne and Gerald both very sympathetic, but had to take turns going out of the room to laugh. How embarrassing! Bet Billy Graham never had to face his public with two bulging bandaged thumbs. Bit of an early set-back really. Can't help feeling nervous about church tomorrow. I know what'll happen – Leonard Thynn will just cackle, Doreen Cook will want to lay hands on my thumbs, and everyone else will be very compassionate and secretly want to ask me how on earth I could've injured *both* thumbs!

Sunday 13 April

What a relief. Edwin rang early to say that there's no church this morning. Gave me a list of names (*my* study-group!) to phone and pass on the news to. Asked him why church was off. He said, "Oh there was a mix-up in the bookings for Unity Hall. Nobody's fault really, but the local caged-bird society have got it for the morning."

When I told Gerald about this, he said, "Oh, it'll be business as usual up at the old hall this morning, then."

Now that I have a position of responsibility in the church, I don't intend to allow this kind of foolish comment from Gerald. Gave him a look that was meant to combine fundamental acceptance with loving but firm chastisement.

Gerald said, "Thumbs giving you stick, eh, Dad?"

Went off to meet Elsie before I could put him straight.

Decided this afternoon that, as a study-group leader, a dramatic improvement is needed in my prayer-life. Intend to pray for two solid hours *every* night after Anne's gone to bed. Two hours should be enough – don't want to overdo it.

1.30 A.M.

So far so good. Prayed from 11.15 until 1.15. Feel tired but mystical. Must keep it up.

Monday 14 April

Rather a shame Anne and Gerald can't make the same efforts over consideration for others as I'm making over prayer. The row they made getting up this morning when I was trying to get a bit of extra sleep! Seems there's a problem with the washing machine, which is playing up. Why they had to discuss it at the tops of their voices is beyond me.

Forgave them.

Seven separate people at work asked how I "did my thumbs". Everett Glander made what can only be described as an unsavoury suggestion about the cause of my injuries. If I wasn't a Christian and a study-group leader I'd push Glander's head through the shredder.

Hope these bandages are off by Thursday!!

About to start my new extra prayer-time this evening, but got distracted by the quarter-finals of the North-East Bedfordshire indoor bowls championship on TV. Suddenly it's 1.00 A.M.! Too tired to pray. Why have I watched bowls instead of praying? I don't *play* bowls! I'm not *interested* in bowls!

Never mind – tomorrow, I'll get it *right*.

Tuesday 15 April

6.00 P.M.

Overheard Gerald on the phone when I got home just now.

"And then, Elsie – *then*, he put the *other* hand in, and – oh! Hello Dad . . ."

If the Bible's right about long life depending on respect for parents, Gerald will be lucky to make it to Saturday, let alone three score years and ten.

2.00 A.M.

Really, truly, honestly, *did* intend to pray tonight. Got caught up in a long Albanian film with sub-titles, set in a kitchen. Kept thinking something was going to happen, but it never did, and suddenly the film finished.

Have crawled to bed. . . .

Wednesday 16 April

Felt exhausted and morose at breakfast.

Anne said, "How's the late prayer going, darling?"

Couldn't meet her eye. "All right," I mumbled.

Gerald said, "Were you speaking in tongues most of the time, Dad? I could have sworn I heard you speaking in Albanian for ages."

Very funny!

Fell asleep at work today.

Leonard Thynn came round this evening while I was asleep in my chair after supper. He drew little faces on my thumb bandages with felt-pen and wrote "Thynn was here" underneath, on both of them. Anne and Gerald just let him! They were all sitting with foolish grins on their faces when I woke up. Thynn can be very silly sometimes. Suggested *all* the members of our study-group should wear bandages on their thumbs, like a secret society. Gerald suggested our theme tune should be "Thumb enchanted evening". Thynn cackled at this, then said he knew a way to cope with problems such as my thumbs. Asked wearily what it was. He told me to go and stand behind the television. Decided to humour him. Stood behind the TV and said, "All right, Leonard, how does this help?"

"Well," said Leonard, "it teaches you how to face set-backs!"

They all roared.

Forgave them.

Thursday 17 April

Was absolutely determined to get the prayer thing right last night. Knelt down at 11.00 P.M. and closed my eyes. Woken and manhandled to bed at 4.00 A.M. by Anne. Didn't seem over-sympathetic really.

Fell asleep at work again. Glander poured ice-cold water on me, then claimed to have raised me from the dead when I sat up at my desk and shrieked.

So tired!!

Got home to find Anne with one of those okay-this-is-going-to-get-sorted-out-right-now expressions on her face.

She said, "Darling, tell me why you can't go to bed early and then get up early to pray."

"Oh," I said, "I don't like getting up . . ."

"Quite!" said Anne. "And I don't like being joined every morning by a guilty, exhausted, disillusioned mystic. Besides . . ."

She smiled shyly.

"I – well, I miss you at night. Couldn't you just *try* the other way? Just for a while?"

Promised I'd try.

10.00 P.M.

My first meeting as a study-group leader is over.

Not a particularly good start to the evening. Apart from feeling exhausted and still wearing my ridiculous bandages, the members of the group seemed to have undergone a mysterious change since last week. Last time we met most of them were pleasant, easy-going people who co-operated with group aims. This week they were awkward, late (some of them) difficult to quieten down when it was time to start, and generally unresponsive.

Really wanted to throttle Thynn, who does tend to wear a joke out. He went up to each person as they came in, and sang "Thumbwhere, over the rainbow . . ." and pointed at me with a stupid smirk on his face.

Wondered why I'd not noticed before what a rebellious crowd of people these are. When we got going at last, I noted that Norma Twill was insufficiently joyful during the choruses, Vernon Rawlings yawned in the middle of the Scripture reading, and Percy Brain had his eyes open during the prayers.

Profound silence for an hour and a half as I delivered a study on "The function of citrus fruit in the Old Testament". Asked if there were any questions at the end. Long, rather disappointing silence, until young Bessie Trench raised her hand.

"Yes, Bessie?" I said, "What's your question?"

Really pleased someone had been listening.

Bessie twisted her fingers together and cleared her throat.

She said, "How did you do your thumbs?"

10.15 P.M.

Going to bed now. Seems ridiculously early, still . . .

Friday 18 April

9.00 A.M.

Up at 6.00 A.M.! Good prayer-time. Glad I decided to switch to the morning. Asked Anne at breakfast why she thought people were deliberately making things difficult for me now that I'm a study-group leader.

She laughed!

"It's not *them* that have changed, darling. It's you! You're a leader now. It's just that all their funny little ways didn't bother you before. Now you notice everything, and you think it's something to do with how they feel about you. They're not there to make *you* feel better, you know; you're supposed to be serving *them*, not the other way round."

Yes . . . well . . . perhaps . . .

Bandages off my thumbs before going to work this morning, thank goodness. No more silly comments. Great!

6.00 P.M.

Small boy stopped me on the way home from work just now.

"Oi, mister! ow come yer fumbs is all white 'n' crinkly, an' the rest of yer 'ands ain't?"

Thursday 24 April

Spent part of my prayer-time this morning thinking about what Anne said on Friday. She's absolutely right! My job is to serve the study-group, not tell them what to do and judge them. From now on I'm going to put myself entirely at the disposal of the members of my study-group, ready and willing to pour myself out for them in every way that's necessary. Hallelujah! Oddly enough, when I expressed all this to Anne, she looked a bit worried. Perhaps when one takes a spiritual step forward (albeit very humbly), as I feel I've done, it's bound to threaten others a little.

Have decided to give a duplicated letter to each of the people in my group tonight offering my services as a Christian friend and counsellor at any time of the day or night. Spent the time between getting home from work and study-group, getting the letter ready, and planning the meeting. Afraid I had to speak a little sharply to Anne once or twice. She's still fretting about the washing machine. I feel that the Lord would not have me troubled with these things at this time.

10.00 P.M.

What an amazing meeting! We were all mightily blessed! (Thynn says he wasn't, but I told him he was in ways that he knows not of.)

My letter received with great enthusiasm. Amazed to find one or two people approached me *this evening* with problems that will need dealing with in the next few days!

There is a world of need! I hear the call! I am ready!

Friday 25 April

Out. New washer: Norma Twill.

Saturday 26 April

Out again. Percy Brain: Doubt.

Sunday 27 April

Church.

Out: Norman Simmonds – furniture moving

Norma Twill – check washer

Deaf old Mrs Thynn – explained that old Mr Verge next-door (who she hit with one of Leonard's Doc Martin ten-holers) said he wanted to "*speak* with her", not "*sleep* with her".

Monday 28 April

Out. Vernon Rawlings: Lust and allied problems.

Tuesday 29 April

Out. Study-group leaders' meeting: (I'm one)

Wednesday 30 April

Out. Stenneth Flushpool: Dominoes while Mrs F. was out. Very excited. (Him I mean)

Thursday 1 May

Out before study-group. Ephraim Trench: Pregnant cow. (Rang me by mistake instead of the vet.)

Great study-group. Planning / talking about the Lord's work. Reminded everybody that I'm always available.

Friday 2 May

Out. George Farmer: Prayer re fruit.

Have had to cut morning prayer right down to save energy for church work in evenings.

Saturday 3 May

Out. Norma Twill: Double check washer.

Sunday 4 May

Church.
Out.

Monday 5 May

Out.

Tuesday 6 May

Out.

Wednesday 7 May

Out.

Thursday 8 May

Out – study-group – out.

Friday 9 May

Out.

Saturday 10 May

First time I've had the chance to write much in my diary for a while. Life is good! Being a study-group leader is a real privilege. Never felt so humble. Constantly busy with pastoral work. Hallelujah!

Sorry to say Anne and Gerald are not totally supportive. Anne seems obsessed by this fault in the washing machine. Can anything be of more importance than the Lord's work?

As for Gerald – if he says "Keep your hair on, Moses" one more time, there'll be trouble.

Sunday 11 May

To church. Can't understand people who don't join in at church. I really question their commitment. Makes life so difficult for us leaders. Gerald didn't come today. Said he was suffering from a pain in the neck and wanted a rest from it. Odd way of putting it!

Anne asked about the washing machine again this evening. Suddenly remembered Percy Brain's earache. Felt led to pop round and pray with him. Stayed late, listening to Percy's theatrical stories. Hilarious! Left, feeling I'd really brought joy into the old boy's lonely life. Home at midnight to find Anne hand washing clothes in the sink.

I said, "Anne, love, Scripture teaches the body is the temple of the holy spirit. Shouldn't this have been done earlier?"

No reply, but something about her back showed she was really listening. Straight to bed. Asleep in seconds.

Monday 12 May

Decorated the Thynn's hall tonight with Leonard. Stayed for Scrabble afterwards. Felt right, as it's a very relationship-building activity.

Back late to find a note from Gerald saying that Roger Forster is an anagram of "Frog restorer". Tore it up. I will not tolerate disrespect in this house!

Tuesday 13 May

About to tackle washing machine when the phone rang. It was young Vernon Rawlings asking what passage we would be studying on Thursday. Dropped everything and said I'd be round immediately to explain.

Anne looked furious. Funny – I thought she liked young Vernon.

Wednesday 14 May

Really annoyed! Gerald's tinkered with the washing machine and made it worse. Reminded him that Scripture says we must be good stewards and not go round causing extra expense by meddling.

A little later, as I was leaving to help the Cooks with young Charles' problem about free will and predestination, I distinctly heard Anne and Gerald arguing in the log shed about who should use the axe first. Curious!

Thursday 15 May

Are Anne and Gerald undergoing a spiritual crisis? I have discerned that their general attitude is cold and unresponsive. Neither of them said anything at the study-group tonight.

Later, while she was washing-up the coffee cups, I said to Anne, "Anne, I think I've got a word for you."

She said, "And I've got one for you if that machine's not soon fixed!"

Prayed for her.

Friday 16 May

6.15

Home at six to find everyone out and a note on the side from Anne, alerting me to the fact that an abandoned family has turned up in

Humph's cafe, just round the corner from us. Could I deal with it? Great! Spiritual adventure! I feel like the Red Adaire of the Christian world. I shall go out now, armed with the Spirit and the Word, to face and do battle with whatever forces of darkness await me!

8.30 P.M.

Got round to Humph's cafe about 6.30, but apart from Humph, the only people in there were Anne and Gerald! They were sitting by a table right at the back, drinking tea. Couldn't think what was going on. Sat down at the table with them. I said, "Where's the abandoned family?"

Gerald said, "We're it."

"But it was just . . . I was just . . . just doing the Lord's work. . . ."

Anne said, "We thought perhaps *we* might be the Lord's work as well – just now and then, if that's all right?"

Gerald bought chips all round. I promised to mend the washing machine. I said sorry. We all laughed. We reckoned God laughed too.

Saturday 17 May

Mended the washing machine this morning. Took seven minutes.

◆━◆

Sacred Diary of Adrian Plass, Christian Speaker,
Aged Thirty-Seven and Three Quarters

THE STUDY

Another of those unexpected parables. This time I obviously needed a reminder of what is really important in my life.

―――――――――

We had just moved house, and for the first time since I began to be a professional writer I had a study, my very own little kingdom. It wasn't a large room; in fact it was quite small, with a little walk-in storage cupboard to one side, but, as I delighted in telling friends who dropped in to look around, it was *mine*. It belonged to me. It was a place dedicated to my use. It wasn't anyone else's. It didn't belong to another person. It was exclusively earmarked for the work that I did. It was *mine*. If I could have thought of another thirty-five ways of expressing that succulent fact, I would have used them to bore my friends to death at an even faster rate than usual. I was *so* happy to have my own space.

One of the first things I did on acquiring my citadel was to hunt through all our books (some were unpacked and on shelves, many were still in the cardboard boxes we used for the move) to find all the "comfort books" that have meant so much to me throughout my life. These included children's books, particularly the "Just William" series by Richmal Crompton, humorous works by giants of literary comedy like P. G. Wodehouse and Jerome K. Jerome, several C. S. Lewis favourites, and a whole other widely varying selection of writings that have enriched my life in one way or another. They're a shabby, overbrowsed bunch all-in-all, a few very unwisely read in the bath, but, for the first time, they were all standing richly together on rows of shelves beside the door, and just behind me as I sat at my desk. No longer would they have to be hunted down with the mounting fury and diminishing patience that has become my very own special trademark.

Because, you see, they were *mine*, and they were in *my* study.

I really enjoyed setting my desk up as well. On the left-hand corner at the back stood the white angle poise lamp that I switch on every morning before starting work, however dark or light the morning might be – nowadays that small action seems to correspond with switching my brain on in some strange way. In the centre of my desk stood the computer, the one that's frequently rude to me, and on the right stood the printer. The printer is in league with the computer, but I have its measure now. Discipline is what works with a printer. Be firm. Simply refuse to accept any hint of failure to operate properly. My wife occasionally uses this machine and regularly has trouble with it because she's too soft. On these occasions she calls me. The moment I appear the cowardly thing flings itself into frantic, chattering, panic-stricken action, hoping to win my approval and avoid a beating. Believe me, you've got to let a printer know who's boss.

At the front of my desk and to the left stands the combination telephone, fax, and answering machine. I endure its leering presence only because I need it so much, but I'm only too aware that it secretly resents finding itself owned by a technological lame-brain like me. Some day the reckoning must come. I'm ready.

In one of the desk drawers beside my chair I squirrelled away a delicious collection of stationery articles which I planned to try very hard never to use. I have always been irresistibly drawn to stationery counters in newsagents' shops. I'm a loony about stationery. I love it all. I love the rubber bands and the sticky labels and the pencil sharpeners and the pencils and the Sellotape and the paperclips and the staple guns and the Blu-Tack and the drawing pins and the neat little packs of envelopes. I love their fiddly, twiddly, functional little beingness, and I love having them stowed away in *my* drawer. Yes, I do! In the other, lower drawer there were just under a million cheap Biros. Resigned to the wretchedly shameful fact that every single member of my family is an incurable pen-thief, I asked only that *one* functional pen should be available when I needed it.

On the shelf to my right, a shelf miraculously fixed to the wall for me by a friend who has the Gift of Attachment, there were two things. The first was a little row of reference books. These were, in no particular order, the *Concise Oxford Dictionary*, a *Complete Concordance* of the New International Version of the Bible, H. L. Mencken's *Dictionary of Quotations*, and a Chambers paperback *Thesaurus*. It's from these volumes that I frequently haul planks to facilitate crossing the yawning chasms of my thought and creativity. They stand beside me as I write today, sturdy forests of wisdom.

The second thing on the shelf was a pot containing three blooming hyacinth plants, bought for me by my wife. This was an act of profound generosity on her part, knowing as she does that buying a hyacinth for me is the equivalent of sending any other man off to Brighton for a weekend with Pamela Anderson. The way in which I wantonly soak in the scent of hyacinths is positively sinful. (I suppose that should be *negatively* sinful, shouldn't it?) I don't know why it is, but that particular heavenly aroma makes my eyes glaze over with pleasure. You can keep your hash and your Ecstasy – I shall stick to my hyacinths. I rather like the idea of clubs full of people with glazed eyes passing pots of hyacinths around.

Other features of my newly appointed little place of work included the chair I'm now sitting on – firm, yet sufficiently yielding in the seat to become formed by the force of gravity into my individual shape as the months went by, and another seat in the corner, not quite so comfortable, of course, for those who would be granted temporary residence in my kingdom from time to time. Add to all these things the walk-in cupboard where, for the first time in living memory, my files were stored in some kind of easily accessible manner, and you could hardly blame me if I began to feel that it would only really be necessary to leave this place in order to have the odd meal and to sleep.

Isn't it funny how God sends little things to teach you a lesson? I came into my study one morning soon after setting it all up, glanced pleasurably around for a moment or two, yet again relishing the fact that it was all *mine*, and sat down at my desk. I think I really had got a little bit carried away with the way in which the whole thing was so organized and self-contained and geared exclusively to what I wanted. Glancing down to my right, where a recently acquired memo board was leaning against the desk-leg waiting to be attached to the wall, I felt a sudden spasm of annoyance. The day before I had very carefully used my specially purchased, wet-wipe pen to make a list of the tasks that had to be performed on the following day. Some *evil* person had rubbed out my list and written something else instead. I was about to storm out and exact summary revenge on the only likely suspect, my ten-year-old daughter, when I happened to notice what had been written across the white surface of the board.

"IMPORTANT," it said, in huge capital letters, and then there was a big arrow pointing to just four little words in the corner. So small were they that I had to get down on my hands and knees to see what they said.

"Remember to kiss Katy. . . ."

May God, in his mercy, grant me the humility and wisdom to remember, when I'm obsessed or caught up with my own possessions and concerns and accomplishments, that the demands of love and relationship will always be a first priority in the only kingdom that really matters.

Thank you, Jesus – and Katy.

•––◆––•

Why I Follow Jesus

HEALED TO
BE YOURSELF

Here is Jesus bringing healing to Peter's family, and demonstrating an important truth at the same time.

> As soon as they left the synagogue, they entered the house of Simon and Andrew, with James and John. Now Simon's mother-in-law was in bed with a fever, and they told him about her at once. He came and took her by the hand and lifted her up. Then the fever left her, and she began to serve them.
>
> That evening, at sundown, they brought to him all who were sick or possessed with demons. And the whole city was gathered around the door. And he cured many who were sick with various diseases, and cast out many demons; and he would not permit the demons to speak, because they knew him.

Mark 1 : 29 – 34 NRSV

How frustrating for Simon's mother-in-law to know that Jesus was in her house and that her fever was making it impossible to get up and look after him. He knew how she was feeling, of course, and do you detect, as I do, a hint of respect and closeness in that little nugget of information about him taking her hand and lifting her up? I know that the phrase is used elsewhere in the gospels, but there is an elegance and, perhaps, an exchanged smile in the middle of all that somewhere.

The lesson that is frequently drawn from this account of the healing of Simon's mother-in-law is about God healing us so that we will then be able to serve him. A perfectly good point to make, of course, but I suspect that there is an even more important lesson to be learned. You see, I have no doubt at all that Simon's mother-in-law was in the habit of serving on a day-to-day basis. It was part of what she was. Being healed simply released her to be herself.

Let us take courage, all those of us who feel that we have been pushed into a strange and alien shape by the expectations of those who see conformity as a priority. Conformity is very far from being the priority of the Holy Spirit. When God heals our bodies or our minds or our spirits, his aim is not to suppress our special characteristics, but to set us free to be ourselves in the best and most useful way possible.

Now that is what I *call* good news.

•—◆—•

Never Mind the Reversing Ducks

WOMAN, BEHOLD
YOUR SON

═══════════

"Words From the Cross" was a joint production by my friend, Ben Ecclestone, and myself. He did the pictures and I wrote the poems, based on the seven speeches that Jesus made from the cross. Here is Mary, standing at the foot of the cross and seeing the broken figure of Jesus through a mother's eyes. There are times when it is essential to think what we think and feel what we feel, especially in relation to family. They are too precious to get stupidly religious over.

═══════════

Today I do not want to be a branch of the vine
Or a part of the body
Or a sheep in the flock of the Good Shepherd
Or the bride of Christ
Or a disciple
Or a servant
Or an inheritor of the Kingdom
Or a citizen of Heaven
Or visited by angels
Or greatly blessed

Or deeply troubled

Or someone else's mother

I just want to get my son down from this wooden thing

And take him home

And make him better

And give him something to eat

And hear him laugh

And persuade him to give up being the Messiah and go back to
carpentry

Words From the Cross

LIVING FOR NOW

C. S. Lewis said that, if the world were to become perfect, God would look down and see a man reading a book in a garden. It has taken me a long time to understand this.

＝＝＝＝＝＝

So-called prosaic or trivial activities happening right now are actually at the heart of real peace and contentment. This awareness might take us a long way towards understanding what Jesus was talking about when he spoke of the kingdom of God actually being among us, and it may also be the key to a special kind of joy that is much deeper and more spiritually nourishing than mere happiness. I suspect that Jesus looked fondly around at the faces of his disciples as they all ate meals together and knew with a sweet mixture of joy and pain that this was as good as it was likely to get on this side of heaven.

These thoughts arose in me on the day following my return from a summer holiday I once spent in France with the other five members of my family. It was a good and enjoyable experience to be away together, despite the occasional (and in our case seemingly inevitable) arguments and tensions, but two things particularly spring to mind in connection with the things that I have just been saying.

The first was a couple of hours spent in the beautiful forest on the hills overlooking a little cottage in Normandy where we stay quite often. We took bicycles with us on the back of the car to ride along the tree-lined tracks, a rug to sit on, a ball to throw, a bottle of orange squash to drink, a big bag of crisps to eat and a book to read. As we sat in the dappled coolness of the cathedral-like forest, throwing our ball to each other and listening as Katy (aged eleven at the time) read to us, I very nearly managed to allow *now* to be eternal.

The other occasion was earlier in the holiday, when we were staying at a place much farther south, quite near to the wonderful city of Chartres. Four of us hired putters and golf balls so that we could play on one of the Crazy Golf courses that the French seem so keen on. We were the only people there because a light rain was falling, and it turned out to be one of those God-given times when the silliest things seem screamingly funny and you don't care whether you win or lose and the weather can do what it likes. We were people who loved each other, being happy for an hour. For me, at least, nothing else mattered. When we returned to the place where we were staying, I wrote the first poem I had written for quite a long time:

> There is not much more
> Need not be more
> Than playing Crazy Golf in France
> Laughing in the summer rain.

Sufficient unto the day is the evil thereof – the good as well, one suspects. Thank God for the *now*.

• ◆ •

Why I Follow Jesus

I WISH I WAS
MY SON AGAIN

One of the most moving aspects of parenthood is watching your children as they discover for the first time, things that have become so familiar that you hardly notice them. I had often prayed that the spirit of excited discovery would not die in my children, as it had in me for so long. When the oldest, Matthew, was five, he and I had taken a walk through the January streets one morning, to get to the park. When we came back, I tried to preserve part of that experience in the following lines.

I wish I was my son again,
The first in all the world to know,
The cornflake crunch of frosted grass,
Beside the polar paving stones,
Beneath the drip of liquid light,
From water-colour, winter suns.

Clearing Away the Rubbish

KATHY'S
BIRTHDAY PARTY

Celebration is definitely a priority. Mike Robinson has organised a big party to celebrate his wife's fiftieth birthday. Kathy is the narrator.

"Right, squeeze in everybody," shouted Mike over the hubbub, "bring your glass with you or grab another one. Make sure there's something in it. Come on, push up at the front and push in at the back. We don't want anyone to end up gnashing their teeth in the hall."

I don't know if Mike pictured everyone sitting in neat cross-legged rows with a grown-up on a chair at the end of each line. If so, he must have been sorely disappointed. Shrieks and squeals of hysterical laughter from those who enjoyed this kind of thing accompanied chaotic efforts by all those present to obey Mike's command, but in the end, by some sacrificial, floor-dwelling, lap-sitting, intertwining miracle of limb-redistribution, the entire assembly was at last corked tightly into the room, and Mike held up a hand for hush.

"Right, I want to start," he said, "by thanking you all very much for your good wishes and your gifts, but thank you most of all for simply being here to help us celebrate Kathy's sixtieth birthday tonight."

I swung my arm stiffly like one of those entry gates in the super-market, hitting him jovially but quite firmly with the back of my fist. Much laughter.

"Sorry, Kath, I meant fiftieth, of course. Time passes so quickly when you're having fun – so I've been told."

More laughter.

"I don't think we've ever had so many friends and family all together at exactly the same time. It really is so lovely to see you all in our home.

So, let's start by giving each other a big round of applause for being here at all."

As people clapped furiously, I scanned the sea of faces before me. The whole world seemed to be squashed into our sitting-room. Jack, Mark, and Felicity were sitting on the floor, more or less at my feet. I could sense a very natural excitement in them, but there was an excitement within their excitement that rather puzzled me.

Carefully selected relatives beamed in my direction from various points in the room (they had been selected on the basis of beaming potential and discretion). Simon Davenport was there, as well as Eileen and the rest of our house-group, together with other friends from the church. The girl who delivered the milk had plucked up her courage and come. There she was now by the door, looking very pretty out of uniform, and happy, if a little confused. Colleagues from Mike's school had come, and folk from the immediate neighbourhood, including the increasingly frail but unquenchably feisty Mrs Van Geeting from next door, a particular across-the-fence favourite with Dip and me. Even Mark's tadpoles were jammed into an impossibly small space in the angle of the wall behind the television in the far corner. Everyone was there, in fact, except – I swept the room with my eyes one more time to make sure – everyone except Dip. She was nowhere to be seen. My heart sank.

"Mike!" I hissed, as the applause began to subside, "Dip's *not* here. She must have got cold feet. I think we should –"

"Dip's fine," he interrupted in a whisper, laying a hand on my shoulder, "trust me!"

So, after looking into his eyes for a moment, and although it didn't make any sense, I trusted him.

"Okay!" Mike clapped his hands together and rubbed his palms expectantly. "Our three children are here in front of us, and before I make my little speech they've all got something to say." Pause. "I'm very proud of my children –"

"Uh-oh!" I interrupted, "joke on the starboard bow – fire at will."

Cheers from many and machine-gun noises from a few.

"No, no, I mean it. We're glad we had Jack, Mark, and Felicity, despite friends advising us early in our marriage that we should avoid having children for the same reason that we shouldn't change our car from petrol to diesel. They told us that, compared with petrol, diesel was noisy, smelly, and lacked acceleration."

Laughter, groans, the odd cry of "Shame!" and a disapproving glare from Felicity, who had reached the age where jokes of that sort had to be about other people. Even a light-hearted suggestion that she might be noisy, smelly, and slow didn't go down at all well. I directed a reassuring, he-was-only-joking smile at her, but she brightened up anyway at Mike's next words.

"I know that Felicity and Jack have something to do for you now, so I'll hand you over to them. Jack and Felicity!"

Amid tumultuous, floor-thumping applause, Jack and Felicity got to their feet and stood on either side of me facing the populous, both clutching a sheet of paper.

"Felicity and I would like to perform a sort of tribute to Mum," announced Jack gravely, as soon as there was quiet.

I sensed everyone gearing up to being deeply moved, but none of them knew Jack as well as I did. I smiled inside and did my level best to look as sombre as my son.

"Yes," said Felicity with equal gravity, "we wrote down all the things about Mum that came into both our heads an' turned them into a poem. Well, Jack did most of the turning, but I helped."

"A serious poem," added Jack, "about a person we deeply respect."

Felicity nodded in earnest agreement, but her whole body was bobbing and quivering infinitesimally with the joy of the moment.

"We're going to read a verse al – ternatively," she said.

"Alternately," corrected Jack.

"Alternately – a verse each at a time."

"That's right, with Flitty starting."

The doggerel that my daughter and her oldest brother then proceeded to recite was so heavily punctuated and interrupted by laughter, cat-calls, and applause that an accurate record of the event itself is virtually impossible. Here, however, is a bald transcription of the verses that they read:

Mummy lives in Daddy's house
She gets all red and cross
She watches *Friends* on telly
and she really fancies Ross.
Mummy says be good at meals
And shouts when we don't do it
She picked a bowl of leeks up once,
And jolly nearly threw it.

Mummy does aerobics,
With some younger, thinner mothers,
She wears long shirts and leggings,
And she hides behind the others.

Mummy told her best friend, Dip,
About her favourite dream,
She falls into a river,
And it's made of Bristol Cream.
Born with three score years and ten,
Of fifty she's bereft,
Or, turned into a fraction,
She's got three sevenths left.
Mummy was a writer once,
She even wrote a book,
But since the "blasted kids" arrived,
She's forced to clean and cook.

For almost half her life on earth,
Our mum has loved us best,
Thank you, Mum, we promise,
We will love you for the rest.

There was no doubting the success of this item. Thunderous appreciation threatened to lift the roof off our faithful old centurion of a house, as Felicity, her face flushed with pleasure and pride, threw her arms around my neck, kissed me on the cheek, and wished me a happy birthday.

I had to check a tear at this point, not, as it happens, in response to the last verse of the poem (I knew all too well that my children loved me), but because of the reference to my writing. This reaction took me by surprise. It was not unlike another moment in the recent past when I had become aware that I was no longer mourning my mother's death with the same suffocating pungency of grief as in the early days after losing her. I had felt ashamed of overcoming the worst of my pain, as though I had let her down,

But this was about writing. I had once been a writer. Now I was fifty, and I was not a writer any more. Okay, I accepted it, but what was I? How do you find out what you are?

I hugged Felicity hard, wishing, as I buried my face in the warm material of her sweatshirt, that my mother could be here at my party, fiddling around endlessly in the kitchen, scolding me for getting het-up, pointing out what was wrong with my life in private and defending me to the death in public. If she could have just – been here. All the old God stuff had jolly well better be right, I thought. I pulled myself together as Mike spoke again.

"Thank you very much, Jack and Felicity. Felicity will be –"

"Hey, hold on," I broke in, "surely I'm allowed say just a word or two in my own defence, aren't I?"

"Mmm, I don't know – well, okay, I'll put it to the vote," said Mike. "All those in favour of Kathy being allowed to say a word or two in her own defence, please raise a hand."

A veritable garden-centre of hands shot up.

"Thank you very much for your kind permission. First of all, I thought it was an excellent poem, and very well read – well done, Felicity and Jack. Having said that, I must insist on salvaging what remains of my good name and my reputation for sanity by pointing out that I most certainly do *not* fancy Ross. As Jack and Felicity know full well, I would regard going out with him as the rough equivalent of marrying my great aunt. When the last trump sounds and all is revealed, the communion of saints on earth and in heaven will learn that his name was only put on the end of the last line because it rhymes with 'cross', an adjective that I suppose might occasionally be applied to me...."

Exaggerated gasps of incredulity from all the members of my immediate family and from one or two others present as well.

"As for the bowl of leeks, I deeply resent the suggestion that I nearly threw it. I *did* throw it – well, I slid it as hard as I could and it would have fallen on the floor if Mike hadn't caught it at the other end...."

Riotous applause, received by Mike with a gracious bow, after which I continued.

"It was an extraordinarily satisfying thing to do, and I would thoroughly recommend it to all those whose children react to the sight of their mother's choicer dishes by sticking their fingers in their mouths and pretending to vomit. As for the rest of the poem, the aerobics, the – what was the other thing? – ah, yes, the sherry dream, only having three-sevenths of my life left, and calling this lot 'The blasted kids' on one or two occasions, I confess to them all, but I absolutely refuse to repent, as it's my birthday. Thank you."

"As I was about to say before I was so predictably interrupted," continued Mike as soon as calm returned once more, "Felicity will be doing one other thing a little later on, but I know that Jack and Mark want to say a few words now."

Jack, still standing beside me, cleared his throat.

"I don't want to say much, just that I love my mum and I hope she has a really good party, and a happy birthday and, most important of all, I hope God forgives her for lying about Ross. Happy birthday, Mumsy."

The smile he gave me before sitting down was a much better speech. I shook my head in wonder. Imagine my first baby becoming a proper grown-up.

I felt quite worried for Mark as he dragged himself to his feet, his dark features unusually pink and nervous. Secretly I was amazed that he had decided to say anything at all in public. This was certainly not his sort of thing, and it can't have been made any easier by the fact that there was a complete absence of noise as he turned to face the room. It was as if all those people somehow sensed the fragility of his confidence and were afraid that a slight sound might kill it altogether. When he did start to speak, it was quietly, and definitely in the manner of one who has abandoned his prepared speech.

"Mum an' I don't always get on."

The silence into which these seven words fell like sparrows' eggs onto a snowdrift, was made to seem even more profound by a very faint hiccup of ten-year-old satirical laughter from Felicity, who was sitting cross-legged on the floor next to me, staring at her ankles. At the back of the room the tadpoles were transfixed behind the telly, rigid with horror as they imagined themselves committing such an appalling act of self-exposure.

"We are sort of like each other really – well, in ways, you know … "

Mark turned towards me, a fierce frown on his face.

"But, it doesn't mean – I mean, just because we sometimes fall out doesn't mean that we don't – you know. I try an' she tries … "

Oh, Mark . . .

"Anyway – happy birthday, Mum."

As Mark put his arms round me and kissed me awkwardly, I realised for the first time what people meant when they talked about "filling up" with emotion. The cumulative effect of the last few days and the things that were happening this evening was pretty powerful. I wasn't keen to overflow in front of all my guests, but I wasn't sure how long I could hold out.

"Just one more thing!" Mike raised his voice and flapped his arms to quell the explosion of approval that had greeted Mark's speech. "Just one more thing before we all go and have some food and get on with the party. First of all, I'd like you all to raise your glasses and drink a toast to Kathy. She and I don't always get on either. . . ."

Comfortable laughter.

"But she's still my sweetheart, and I really do love her very much. Kath, darling, I wish you the happiest birthday of your whole life. To Kathy!"

"To Kathy!" echoed the assembly.

• ◆ •

Stress Family Robinson -The Birthday Party

CAMP
COMMUNION

Camping as a family is a real joy – isn't it? Well, it is sometimes. Here is Adrian the diarist again, recording the worst and the best of open-air living.

Monday 19 May

Reminded by Anne this morning that it's only six days until we set off for our annual trip to "Let God Spring into Royal Acts of Harvest Growth", the big Christian festival down at Wetbridge in the West Country. A whole group of us are going from the church. Rather looking forward to it this year. Other years we've rented caravans. This year we've bought a tent! Can't wait! Bacon sizzling deliciously on the Primus every morning – the healthy feel of open-air living – soft talk under the stars each evening – good fellowship with other campers and caravanners – marvellous! Roll on Saturday!

I've insisted that we leave *very* early, probably about 4.00 A.M. Gerald groaned and Anne sighed when I said this, but it's the *only* way to do it. Up with the lark!

Wednesday 21 May

Said to Anne and Gerald this evening, "*What* time are we leaving on Saturday?"

"Seven, wasn't it?" said Gerald.

"Eight o'clock?" said Anne.

"Four!" I said "F-O-U-R, FOUR!"

Friday 23 May

9.30 P.M.

Early to bed tonight so as to be up and ready to go at 4.00 A.M. I've set the clock for 3.30 A.M., and that's when we're *all* getting up. Gerald smiled that infuriating smile at me just now as he went off to bed. He thinks I'm going to mess it up – set the clock wrong or something. Anne looks pretty sceptical as well. We shall see. Roll on tomorrow morning. This is the one thing that *won't* go wrong!

10.30 P.M.

Having a little trouble getting to sleep because of worrying about waking up.

11.30 P.M.

Still can't get to sleep. Bit worried now. If I don't go off soon I shall sleep right through the alarm. Must try not to try to relax.

12.15 A.M.

Still awake! Only three and a half hours until the alarm goes off!

12.19 A.M.

Dozed off for one and a half minutes. Dreamt I was awake, and woke up worried about not being asleep.

1.00 A.M.

Too late to think about sleeping now, I must stay awake until 3.30. I must!! Going down to the kitchen to drink coffee.

2.00 A.M.

Still awake! Eyes heavy and blurred – all I want to do is sleep. Hour and a half to go. Mustn't lie down – that would be fatal!

2.45 A.M.

I think I'm going to make it. Feel like death but I'm still asleep – I mean awake.

3.00 A.M.

Good as made it, can't stop yawning but swill atake wade awike . . .

3.29 A.M.

Made it! That'll show 'em. Just sitting in the armchair for a moment till the alarm goes off dun it! What a trium . . .

Saturday 24 May

11.00 A.M.

There are times when my family is insufferable! Anne and Gerald woke me at ten o'clock, and pretended to be very upset because we hadn't made an early start. Gerald said I might at least have gone to bed and *tried* to sleep instead of sitting up all night and dozing off in the armchair. Anne said it was no use my having a quiet-time because God had set off for Wetbridge hours ago. Very funny I don't think. Felt like a dead slug when I tried to get out of my armchair. Feel a lot better now I've had a wash and something to eat. Wetbridge here we come! We're meeting the others down there. Must make sure I take my diary along. I'll be able to sit quietly outside the tent each evening and record the events and revelations of the day. Can't wait!

10.00 P.M.

Arrived at "Let God Spring into Royal Acts of Harvest Growth" around mid-afternoon. Anne and Gerald and I erected our new "Tornado-Tough" frame tent in no time, despite high winds and sheeting rain. After checking out the toilets, we walked up to the shop. Passed our magnificent new tent, standing tall and proud in the face of the gale. A little farther on, our magnificent new tent passed us, flying through the air like a huge, loony, red and blue sail. Caught it eventually, just outside Richard and Doreen Cook's Super-Safari-complete-Comfort-Vacation-Van. Could see Richard inside, drinking tea and reading a Bible in the warm. He nodded and smiled and mouthed the words "Praise the Lord" at me, as I wrestled with my horrible pile of soggy canvas.

Mouthed something back.

Everything soaked! Down to Wetbridge launderette to dry it all. Too late to pitch the tent again when we got back. Went to the "Let God Spring into Royal Acts of Harvest Growth" office, where a wild-eyed person (who kept saying this was the last year she'd do it) gave us the key to a tiny refrigerated cowshed, where we're about to stay the night in strange contorted positions.

Sunday 25 May

Down to Wetbridge launderette with clothes soaked by rain coming in through holes in the refrigerated cowshed. Surprising number of people down there at 7.30 in the morning. One couple who'd spent the night in six inches of water were anxious to get back in time for the marriage fulfilment seminar. Seemed a bit desperate really.

Got back and pitched the tent again. Drove pegs through anything that flapped.

Off to the first Celebration this evening with our church group. Relieved Leonard Thynn of a three-pint can of bitter and two bottles of Valpolicella on the way. Explained to him what this kind of Celebration means.

Pleased to see Gerald concentrating hard during the talk. Turned out all his mental energies had gone into working out that Lyndon Bowring was an anagram of "Born lying down". Got a bit annoyed with him.

Monday 26 May

Forgot to put clothes away properly last night. All soaked. Down to Wetbridge launderette again. They should have a seminar *there*.

Pete Meadows spoke tonight. Gerald said afterwards, "Now that was a really good talk, Dad."

Guiltily confessed that I'd spent most of the time working out that Pete Meadows is an anagram of "Sweated poem".

Tuesday 27 May

Back from the Wetbridge launderette this morning to find deaf old Mrs Thynn waiting to tell me how disappointed she was that they hadn't had the chance to save anyone from drowning in her seminar yet.

Stared blankly at her.

"But aren't you in the house-to-house visitation seminar?" I asked. "That's right," she said, "mouth-to-mouth resuscitation."

Honestly! You'd think Leonard would have explained, wouldn't you?

Some problems over *my* seminar this morning. Was to be in Marquee 9, but had been changed to Marquee 6, only Marquee 6 had blown down, so Marquee 9's seminar was moved to Marquee 14, and the new Marquee 6's seminar was moved back to Marquee 9, only, by now, Marquee 9 had also blown down. Our group ended up wandering disconsolately round the site, looking for an empty marquee, and discussing stability in the church as we went.

Overheard two fellow campers in a local shop later on, while I was waiting to buy fruit-gums for the evening talk. One said the bad weather and the tents blowing down was God's way of saying that these huge gatherings were wrong. The other said it was God's way of testing our perseverance in something that was unquestionably *right*. The old local chap behind the counter interrupted them to say that it always "bloody rained" down here at this time of the year, and he couldn't understand why they "kept on 'aving it!"

Wednesday 28 May

Same good old crowd down at Wetbridge launderette this morning. Asked everybody if they'd come to "Let God Spring into Royal Acts of Harvest Growth" again. They all said they would, because the church thrives under persecution.

Back to the site. Went down for a wash. Funny washing in front of strangers every morning. Feel obliged to be a bit more thorough than usual, in case they think I don't wash enough. The water's so *cold*, despite the fact that the taps are labelled "C" and "H". Gerald says that "C" stands for "Cold", and "H" stands for "Horribly Cold".

Thursday 29 May

What a night! Felt as if Giant Haystacks and Big Daddy were shaking our tent in shifts all night. About 2.00 A.M. I said to Anne, "One of us ought to get out and check the guys and pegs, you know."

Anne said, "I agree absolutely. One of us quite definitely should. Yes, one of us should certainly get out and do that."

Rather obvious snore from Gerald's compartment at this point.

Got up eventually and crawled into the darkness to face Giant Haystacks and Big Daddy. Everything secure. Anne and Gerald fast asleep when I got back. Had two nightmares when I finally got to sleep. In the first, I died and went to heaven and found it was just like "Let God Spring into Royal Acts of Harvest Growth". Woke terrified.

In the second, I died and went to hell, and it was just like "Let God Spring into Royal Acts of Harvest Growth". Woke up sweating, and got up early to start collecting stuff for the launderette.

Talked to lots of nice people this morning from lots of different denominations. Had a really great chat in the cafe. Had to stop, unfortunately, or we'd have been late for the seminar on unity.

Friday 30 May

Everything dry this morning! Rather missed the usual launderette trip. Nearly went anyway. . . .

Asked Anne this afternoon if she'd enjoyed it all.

She said, "Oh, yes. Despite everything, it's good to be among all these people who are doing their best to do what God tells them. We're a funny old crowd though, aren't we?"

"Yes," I thought, "we certainly are that."

Silently asked God to show me what really mattered in this strange world of tents and caravans, and Big-tops blowing down, and Celebrations and Christians and cold water and foul weather. As I opened my eyes, a figure passed our tent on the road. It carried a huge wooden mallet. The walk was a plodding, weary one. The young man was dishevelled and grimy. He'd probably been up for the last twenty-four hours at least, working all night in the wind and the rain to save some of the marquee tents. There was the faintest of nightlights still shining in his eyes as he walked. Somehow knew the weather would never quite put that light out.

"There you are," God seemed to say, "That's what it's all about."

It was a steward.

Saturday 31 May

Camp communion today. As we sat waiting for the bread and wine to come round, couldn't help looking at Leonard and Richard and Gerald and Anne and Edwin and the others, and wondering why God's brought us all together. I'm glad he did, though. Felt quite a lump in my throat as I saw old Thynn screwing his eyes tight shut as he took the cup in his hands and sipped his problem and its solution.

Talking of Leonard – that reminds me. Straight after this I'm going to grab him and make him tell me why he's been borrowing our blinking cat....

Sacred Diary of Adrian Plass, Christian Speaker,
aged Thirty-Seven and Three Quarters

Part Five

POWER OF THE PAST

For better or worse the past is the author of the present. Having worked with difficult and disturbed children for years, I know how difficult it is to deal with the echo of negative experiences from early years. I have known these difficulties in my own life. I also know the power of positive influences and memories, and I thank God for all those who brought grace and generosity and love into my life as I was growing up. Without those precious gifts I might not have survived. We bring a lot of baggage into family life, some useful and some potentially destructive. That's what this section is about.

MOTHERS

Learning To Fly was another Ecclestone/Plass production. It was a labour of love, as we very indulgently only included topics and ideas that particularly appealed to us.

This extract is about mothers. My mother was definitely one of the positive influences in my life.

Ben's mother was ninety-five years old when she died. Grace Ecclestone had a deep, uncomplicated belief in God that easily survived her son's occasional hectoring bursts of theological exposition. Frustrating though these useless debates were at the time, Ben now remembers the simple solidity of his mother's faith with warmth and gratitude. He also remembers that she went out to scrub floors after her husband died in order to raise money for fees when he was a student at the Canterbury College of Art.

Handy with a pudding spoon when Ben was an annoying small boy, and famous for her heavy hints in later life, Grace would have given and done anything for her children because she loved them beyond anyone else, except perhaps that very simple God who received her without theological debate as one of his own in June of 1990.

Ben was there when she died. He says it was one of the most peaceful events he's ever witnessed. Her breathing stopped and she slipped quietly from sleep to death.

My own mother was still alive, though confined to a wheelchair, when I wrote this poem.

I remember when my father said
"You'll drive your mother mad if you're not good"

That night I dreamed I had
I saw her sitting on a chair in some sad cell
Nodding, grinning, knowing no one, driven mad indeed
Lost forever to the wicked child who turned her mind
By being bad
The horror woke me
In the dark my thoughts were white and scraped and raw
I had to call her in to sit beside me looking safely sane
I silently resolved I would be good for ever more
And was – all night.

I remember when I learned at school
Just how the hornbeam leaf can be distinguished from the elm
I told my mother
"With the hornbeam, one side starts a little further down, you see"
She seemed to be so fascinated
Said how she would need to see this for herself
Next day, although a crashing, blowing, soaking storm had
   broken out
I ran into the woods when school had ended
Searching frenziedly for hornbeam trees and elms
As the weather beat me up I may have cried
But there was so much wet about
I only know I streamed with it and didn't care.
How excited she would be to see it for herself
The way in which the hornbeam is distinguished from the elm
When I got home I'd caught a chill and had to go to bed
But downstairs in the lounge my trophy twigs stood proudly in
   a vase
And stayed there long beyond the time when they were dead.

And I remember all those nights
When I, a pasty teenage renegade
Came creeping home way past the fury hour

No sound, no lights, no comfort for an unrepentant prodigal like me
Except that when I reached out gently in the dark
I'd find a little pile of Marmite sandwiches
And touch the chilly smoothness of a glass of milk
My mother put them there because the life of God in her
Gave gifts with all the passion of a punishment
To those she loved beyond reproach
Marmite and milk still comfort me.

And I remember all the pain my mother felt
Through years of staring at a mirror telling vicious lies
About the optimistic child in her
So sad
That so much happiness was spilled and wasted
Drained and lost
Until at last the mirror cracked, and, being on her own
She suddenly remembered who she was
Though God and me – we'd always known.

Learning To Fly

THE MOST
EXCITING THING

What are the roots of excitement? As you will see in the following memory from my childhood, this happens to be a very good way of putting the question.

I was in a group that was being asked to talk about the experience that had excited each of us more than any other. It was a Christian group, and, therefore, for better or worse, most of our answers tended to be about conversion or baptism or healing or something similar. One or two people did mention things like hang-gliding and the birth of their children, but in the main spiritual adventures dominated. I didn't say anything for a long time, because I was trying as hard as I could to answer the question. It was very hard to pin down the truth.

Our thrilling three-day stay in the Kruger National Park while we were working in South Africa? That experience could easily have been it, but I knew it wasn't.

Seeing my children born? Mind-blowing, but – no.

First kiss? Definitely not.

Getting married? Too frightening.

Moving into our first house? Not really.

No, it was something else, and the fingertips of my memory were just managing to touch the extreme edge of whatever this thing was. Something further back than those other experiences, something so vibrantly, electrifyingly exciting that the very aura of this unidentified recollection set my nerves tingling and jingling in anticipation of – *what*, for goodness sake?

"Radishes!"

My sudden triumphant cry was received by the rest of the group as though I had uttered some sort of vegan swear word.

"Radishes," I repeated, "my most exciting experience of all time was seeing my radishes come up when I was about three."

Of course it was. Nothing had come close to it since. I remembered it all now. I could see the small square of garden at the edge of my father's allotment, the one that was especially mine. I could see myself carefully making a groove in the earth with a stick, then sowing seeds from the packet that I'd bought at the shop in the village where they seemed to sell everything under the sun. On the back of that packet was a picture illustrating the Platonic ideal of radishness, a bunch of enormous radishes, a luxuriant, emerald growth sprouting from crimson red tops that merged into creamy white at the base. That was how *my* radishes were going to look.

After covering up the seeds with earth I impaled the empty packet in two places on a stick as I had seen my father do, and stuck the stick into the ground at the end of the row, just in case, by some miracle much greater than the miracle of plant production, I should forget what I was growing there. I think also, I had a vague and strictly private notion that the plants might appreciate some kind of reminder of what they were supposed to be as they emerged from the earth.

Kneeling by my newly planted row, I would study the length of raised earth intently, hoping that if I hung around for a few minutes more I might actually spot the very first tiny spot of green appear as the pioneers of my crop struggled towards the light.

For part of every day I squatted by that bed, checking my radishes, becoming very slightly agnostic about the promised metamorphosis as time went by. Then – oh, the indescribable joy of discovering one morning that minuscule green shoots had begun to appear in exactly the right places, the places where little me had ordained that they should appear by sowing the seeds in that very nearly straight line just a few days ago. The promise had come true – things *did* grow!

As all ex-radish enthusiasts will clearly remember, in the early stages of growth a radish plant consists of two tiny oval leaves pushing out in opposite directions, for all the world, I used to think, like two tiny little hands extended in such a manner that each plant seemed to be saying,

"Well, here I am!" I believe I only just stopped short of naming each radish individually.

All I dreamed of from that first day of visible growth was harvest. I was terribly impatient. Days went by. At the first sign of embryonic red globes emerging from the earth I wanted to pull my radishes up. I so wanted to pull my radishes up! I was restrained by higher authority, but only just.

"What if they grow too much?" I inquired worriedly. "What if they grow right up out of the ground and fall over and get eaten by – by cats?"

"Cats don't eat radishes."

"Oh."

At last the shining day arrived. Higher authority decreed that some of my radishes might be ready for pulling up. There can be few more profound and innocently sensual experiences than harvesting your own crop from the rich earth. And, at three, or any other age really, can there be a greater thrill than to walk into your own kitchen, as casually as you can in view of the fact that you are positively shivering with delight, to present your own mother with the first fruits of your own labour? Real, proper teatime on that first day of harvest featured *my* radishes.

I was so proud.

The planning, preparation, daily attention, and eventual reaping of our personal harvest for God needs to be conducted in exactly the same spirit of wonder and innocent excitement that I experienced as a child with my garden. Our limited contribution to the needs of the Kingdom of God may appear small to us, but I can assure you that, if we offer them in the right spirit, they will be taken from our hands with the same seriousness and gratitude that my mother showed when she took those radishes from me when I was three, and which Jesus himself must have shown when, two thousand years ago, he took two loaves and five small fishes (and a couple of radishes?) from a small boy on a hillside.

● ◆ ●

When You Walk

GRAFFITI

It's not easy to shake off the past. Wouldn't it be wonderful if conversion brought immediate repair and transfiguration? Instant perfection. A bit of a shock for our nearest and dearest, though. Imagine waking up to find that "Our Fred", whose every vice is as familiar as an old friend, has become a blazing torch of eternal light. Perhaps it wouldn't be quite so wonderful after all.

But why does the process of change take so long? Why are the labour pains of being born again so prolonged and acute for so many Christian people?

I have a friend whose ministry of healing and counselling has been stunningly effective. He is the smile on the face of God to a procession of needy people, but as his life goes on he is discovering layer upon layer of injury and pain related to the past, particularly in connection with his early years when he suffered sexual abuse from his mother and a very unhappy childhood generally.

Many of his buried memories have been uncovered and healed, but there are many more to come. How can we understand this process by which the past puts painful clamps on the present? Let me suggest just one way to look at it. It can be summed up by the word "graffiti".

The prophet Jeremiah announced God's intention to write his law on the hearts of his people, and the apostle Paul described the Corinthian Christians as a letter from Christ, written on the tablets of human hearts.

The problem though, assuming your heart is anything like mine, is that the negative graffiti accumulated over the years are so thick and indelible that there's not a great deal of space left for anything else.

The devil wields a pretty effective infernal aerosol can. Let me tell you about some of the scribbles I've discovered.

When I was a little boy of six I decided that I wanted to be an actor when I grew up. I announced this intention to an aunt who happened to be staying at the time.

"Oh, no," she replied with sparkling auntly wit, "you have to be good-looking to do that."

Of course, Aunt Gertrude, or whatever her name was, had no intention of upsetting me – she was just being funny. But it's really and truly no exaggeration to say that the discovery that I was not good-looking wounded my self-image for years.

The next scribble – scraped out in capital letters, this one – happened when I was a teenager. I was in the middle of a combined Drama and GCE course at a college of further education in Tunbridge Wells.

One afternoon, as I sat talking to a couple of other students on the lawn at the back of the building, one of the lecturers strolled over and, quite gratuitously, told me that I was a waster. Whatever chances and opportunities came my way, he said, I would misuse and simply waste. Then he strolled off.

I think he was trying to be helpful, but, as we all know, the road to hell is paved with good intentions – or unposted letters in my wife's case – and those few words of his came very close to snuffing out the tiny spark of confidence that glowed faintly in my very insecure teenage heart.

Over the years that sentence has haunted me, and it has never had a constructive effect. It has often weakened my resolve, and still does occasionally.

Sometimes the graffiti are in the form of conversational ruts, the same sort of verbal dialogue repeated again and again, eroding self-confidence and casting a shadow of defeat over the future.

Consider this scene, for example, between a daughter and her father.

DAUGHTER: Did you manage to get my bike done, Dad?

FATHER: I'm changing this plug for your mother, I've just mended the chair that your brother broke, and I've had your Auntie Phyllis on the phone for twenty minutes about next Wednesday. No, I have not got round to doing your bike yet, and it's no good going on about it because I just haven't had time.

DAUGHTER: I didn't mean you should have done it, Dad. I was just asking.

FATHER: Everyone's just asking. I've told you I'll do it, and I will do it just as soon as I can, so you'll just have to be patient.

DAUGHTER: I don't mind being patient, Dad. I wasn't complaining about you not doing it, I was just wondering if you had got round to it. It was just – information I wanted.

FATHER: Okay! All right! I'll leave the plug. Let's not bother about what anyone else wants. Let's just get your bike fixed then you'll be all right and we can start seeing to other people's needs.

DAUGHTER: But I don't want you to do my bike now. I told you, I was just –

FATHER: Well, if you don't want me to do your bike now, why have you been getting so het-up about it?

DAUGHTER: I haven't been getting het-up about it! I wasn't anything when I first came in!

FATHER: Well, what are you shouting at me for if you're not het-up?

DAUGHTER: I *wasn't* het-up!

FATHER: Well, you certainly are now, aren't you? Or is this what you call being calm and peaceful?

DAUGHTER: Dad, when I first came in I simply asked you quite quietly and nicely whether you'd done my bike or not. That's all I wanted to know – had you done my bike.

FATHER: Well, have you moved all your books off the landing yet?

DAUGHTER: No, but that's not what we're talking about!

FATHER: Oh, I see! We're allowed to talk about me not having done what you wanted, but we're not allowed to talk about you letting me down. Don't you think that's a bit less than fair?

DAUGHTER: (*after a pause*) That's stupid, Dad!

FATHER: Ah! Now we come to it, don't we? We usually end up with me being stupid don't we? Do you know what my father would have said to me if I'd ever *dared* to talk to him like that?

DAUGHTER: I –

FATHER: Well, do you?

DAUGHTER: (*dead tones*) Yes I do. You've told me about thirty-nine times. He'd have taken all your privileges away for the next two weeks, and you might have got the strap as well.

FATHER: There's no need to be sarcastic about your grandfather. At least he never set out to cause trouble in the family. He was a good man who never did less than his best. He loved you kids when you were little, and I'd be ashamed to have him standing here listening to the way you're going on! I don't know why you do it! I don't know what's happened to you! We used to play games and have a laugh together. You used to look up to me and ask questions, and I'd show you how to do things – we were best friends dammit! What have I done to deserve you drifting off into being miss Clever-clever?

DAUGHTER: Dad – please! It's not fair. I didn't start any of this!

FATHER: Oh, you didn't start it. Who did then? The man in the moon? You come in here demanding that I do your blessed bike, you tell me that I'm stupid when I talk about other peoples needs, you mock your grandfather who's dead and can't defend himself, and then you tell me you didn't start it. Well I'm sorry but I think I'm too stupid to understand that, much too stupid!

DAUGHTER: (*almost breathless with hurt*) Look Dad, I came in right? And I said – exactly like this – I said, "Have you managed to do my bike, Dad?" and you got all exasperated and went on about all the other things you had to do, but I – wasn't – complaining. I – was – just – asking . . .

FATHER: Yes, like I've just been asking you for weeks and weeks to clear your books and stuff off the landing and help your mother round the house and think about others a bit more than you do –

DAUGHTER: (*furious*) That's not what we were talking about! That's not what we were talking about! You stupid stupid man! You don't want to understand! You don't want to listen to what I'm saying! I didn't start it! I didn't start it! I didn't start it! (*she continues to shout those three words over and over again*)

FATHER: *(calls his wife)* Sheila! Come and lend a hand. Dorothy's having one of her does again.

I could make a long list of the graffiti that clutter my heart space. So could you. Things people have said, failures that have destroyed confidence, traumatic experiences, profound, unforgettable embarrassments – all sorts of things. Usually each one tells you a lie about yourself:

> You will never succeed.
> You are not lovable.
> God has cast you aside because of *that* sin.
> You're boring.
> People will only ever use you.
> Happiness is impossible.
> Your life has no purpose.

The almost invariable untruthfulness of these scrawlings should be sufficient indication of their ultimate authorship. The father of lies is anxious that our souls should be covered by a confused mass of misinformation, some of it so deeply scored that it comes close to breaking our hearts.

Jesus promises that we shall all be washed as white as snow. This may involve several years work by the divine cleaning department in the case of you and me, but we have the promise and therefore we have the hope as well.

◆

View From a Bouncy Castle

THE "TROUBLES"

This and the following reading are from a book called *The Growing Up Pains of Adrian Plass*, which was actually the first book that I ever wrote. Why I should have thought that anyone would be interested in autobiographical details at that stage in my life is a bit of a puzzle, but then a lot of the decisions I make are a bit of a puzzle.

The Holy Spirit has done a lot of healing in my life, but it still causes me great pain to read the following two extracts.

Early photographs show that I was little more than a huge pair of ears mounted on two long skinny legs. In most of those early pictures I look slightly troubled and very earnest.

Each week I attended the local church at the other end of the village, an activity that seemed to me to have very little to do with God. The Roman Catholic chapel in Rusthall was a converted private house and, therefore, lacked the atmosphere of sublime mystery and divine confidence that I rather enjoyed on our occasional visits to St Augustine's, the huge and ornate mother church in Tunbridge Wells.

There were few points of interest for a small child in an hour spent in one of three physical postures, listening to someone speaking a language that he didn't understand, to a God who seemed as distant and irrelevant as the dark side of the moon. Some of those services seemed to be several days long. Afterwards, my father, my two brothers and I would proceed sedately back along the path into the village, all my little springs of boredom and tension popping and pinging into relaxation as I looked forward to Sunday lunch and the traditional midday comedy half-hour on the radio.

Nowadays I have a great respect and fondness for the Roman Catholic Church and many friends who are members of it, but if you had asked me at the age of eight or nine to tell you what I enjoyed most about the Mass, I could have named only one thing. I did rather look forward to that point in the proceedings when the priest placed a wafer in the open mouths of the communicants, as they knelt in a semicircle around him. There was a satisfyingly repellent fleshiness about all those extended tongues and a fascinating vulnerability about the grown-ups, waiting like baby birds to be fed with something that, once inside them (I was told), would turn into the body of Jesus Christ and nourish them in a way that I couldn't begin to understand.

That the church seemed to me to have very little to do with God may have had something to do with the fact that, while my father was a convert to the Catholic Church, my mother, whose religious background was the Congregational Church, remained a Protestant and didn't come to church with us on Sundays.

We frequently experienced our own domestic version of "The Troubles", and I can recall how, as a small child, I felt painfully bewildered about the religious separation between my parents.

Why didn't mummy come to church with us? Did she know a God? No? Well, in that case why didn't she come to church with us? I would understand when I was older, I was told.

The shadow of conflict darkened those Sunday morning services throughout my early childhood and had a strongly negative effect on my feelings about God, who clearly wouldn't or couldn't sort out our family.

My father was a very jealous man. He found it almost impossible to believe that he was loved and wanted by those closest to him. Happiness and peace were just clever devices designed to lull him into a state where he could more easily be cheated and victimised, especially by his wife – my mother – who was one of the most loving and innocent people I have ever met. People outside the family were "all right". They could never give him things that he feared losing in the same way. It was us, the family, and my mother particularly, who were obliged to trip and stumble through the dark forest of his fear and insecurity. In the middle of a pleasant family walk, when it seemed impossible that anything could go wrong, he would quite suddenly stop, and with that expression of tight-lipped anger on his face, that we all dreaded, announce that we were going back.

"Why, Dad?"

"Ask your mother."

My mother, it usually transpired, had "looked" at a man passing along on the other side of the road or working in a field or sitting on a gate or driving a car. This kind of innocent glance was enough to shatter my father's self-esteem and send him into a brooding, sulky state for hours or days or even weeks. Eventually my mother would find a way to bring him round, but only by accepting and playing out the role of penitent, which was a very risky business, as he would only accept her penitence if she was innocent as well. He saw rivals everywhere. The man who came to build the extension onto our kitchen was, he told me, a "naughty" man.

"What do you mean?"

"I'll tell you when you're older."

"Why can't you tell me now?"

"It's not very nice."

The man who took us for catechism lessons in a tall dark room in St Augustine's presbytery was also on the list of suspects. He was a big man with a large, impressive moustache, a profound understanding of the catechism, and an almost total inability to communicate it to children. He was also, so my father said, not a good man.

"Bad, you mean?"

"Yes, very bad."

"What's he done?"

"You wouldn't understand."

"I would!"

"I'll tell you when you're older . . ."

There were so many things that I was going to be told when I was older! So many little clouds of half-knowledge were massing around my understanding, shutting out the light until much later in my life.

The most painful instance of my father's insane jealousy (most painful from my point of view, that is) happened just before my tenth birthday. I arrived home one afternoon after playing some sort of tracking game through the bracken up on the common. Tired, hot, and hungry, I came through the back door into the kitchen and was about to get a drink of water and a wedge of the all-sustaining bread and marmalade, when I heard my father's raised voice coming from the other side of the dining room door. My very heartbeat seemed to fade, as it always did when I realised that "it" was happening again. What now? I opened the door and slipped quietly into the room, thinking vaguely that I might be able to protect someone from something. My mother was shaking her head tearfully, sobbing out the words, "It's just not true, it's just not true!"

My father, with an odd mixture of pain, anger, and relish filling his face and voice, was jabbing his finger towards her and shouting, "I saw you! I saw you with him! I looked through the window and saw you on the bed with him!"

My sympathy fluttered around the room like a nervous butterfly, uncertain where to alight, unsure where to lend the tiny weight of its concern.

"You can't have done – you really can't have done! It's not true . . . !"

Despite ample evidence from the past that plain denial was an absolute waste of time, my mother continued her tearful protest, until my father, suddenly inspired, took a step forward and pointed at me.

"Adrian was with me. He saw it too! Didn't you?"

There was a wild plea in his eyes.

My mother was crying.

They were my parents. You should support your parents. My father was appealing to me to lie for him. My mother needed me to tell the truth. Someone was going to be let down, and we were all going to suffer anyway. My voice was very small as I answered.

"I wasn't with you. I didn't see anything."

I don't think I looked at my father's face. I had failed him by telling the truth. I was a cold mess inside. Angry, unhappy, and of course – guilty.

As an adult, I have come to understand how profoundly my father suffered through his inability to believe in happiness, and I am now able to offer him posthumous forgiveness and feel more peaceful about the past. There is no doubt, though, that the development of my perception of God as a father was sadly distorted by the way in which he presented himself to me both as a Christian and a parent. It is fortunate that my mother was able to provide warmth and consistent care throughout my childhood, and for that I shall always be grateful.

Growing Up Pains of Adrian Plass

MY FATHER'S
PRAYER BOOK

If my poor father had been a more secure man the boredom of the services and even the parental conflict over religion might not have mattered too much. As it was, his inability to trust the love of his family resulted in twenty-five very difficult years for my mother and, in my case, a very confused and troubled perception of what love, adulthood, and Christianity meant. One incident springs to mind as being typical of the kind of emotional half-nelson that he was expert in applying and which must have contributed heavily to the emotional constipation that led to a breakdown in my own life years later in 1984, and from which I am only just emerging as I write.

It concerned my father's black prayer book, a small, plump, much thumbed little volume, whose wafer-thin pages were edged with gold. As a child it seemed to me a miniature treasure chest, filled with immense wealth that had somehow been compressed into a tiny space for easy portage.

Dad's prayer book was part of him, like the little round boxes of Beecham's pills, the tin full of old and foreign coins, the trilby hat, and the tortoise-shell reading spectacles that made my sight worse when I was allowed to try them on, before they were put away again in the case that snapped shut with a pleasing hollow "plock!" sound.

One day we had all been naughty – all three of us. One of my brothers was two years older than I, the other was two years younger. I must have been about eight years old at the time. We seemed to spend our lives pursuing one of three activities. The first involved the consumption of vast slices of white crusty bread, spread thickly with butter and marmalade. We often accounted for three long loaves in a single day. The second activity was simply playing together, and the third, which usually grew naturally out of the second, was simply fighting each other.

Today, the eating and playing stages had passed all too quickly. We three boys had argued and squabbled and cried and fought for most of a long rainy Saturday. My parents' patience had been tried and tested in a way that, with three boys of my own, I now fully understand. They had tried everything: the gentle rebuke, the not-so-gentle rebuke, the appeal to reason, the bribe, the threat, the repeated threat, the repeated-yet-again threat, the last chance option, and finally the shriek of fury. Nothing had worked. My father had long since abandoned any attempt to play an adult role in the proceedings. He was an angry child, hurt by our refusal to make it easy for him to be grown-up. His idea of an appropriate solution to this problem was bizarre, to say the least. He picked up his prayer book from its place next to the biscuit barrel on the sideboard and, holding it dramatically over his head, announced that if we didn't behave ourselves, we would drive him to the point where he would be forced to throw it at us, and if he had to do *that,* it really would be "the end".

Children believe things.

The end of what? Pictures flashed through my mind of the little book, stuffed with condensed divinity, crashing to the floor, bursting like some ripe, heavy fruit, and losing all its goodness for ever. Was that what he meant? Would I be to blame for that? Had I said or done something in the course of that long day of bickering that was more serious – more wicked than I had realised? When he did finally, with a sort of orgasmic zeal, fling the book in the general direction of my younger brother and me, I was surprised to find that the world seemed unaffected by the gesture. No thunderbolts – no voice from heaven. The book lay, almost unharmed, on the floor, one or two pages detached by the impact and protruding slightly from the others, but otherwise, just the same.

I wasn't just the same though. I had made my father throw his prayer book at me, and he had said that it would be "the end". That book contained God. I had made him throw God away.

The devils grinned as they snapped home the padlock on another chain of guilt.

POSITIVE
GRAFFITI

On the other hand. . .

I have discussed elsewhere the way in which Satan uses his infernal aerosol spray to cover our hearts with graffiti. Jeremiah said that God will write his law on our hearts, but where these devilish scrawlings are too deep and too numerous to be easily erased, it can be a very long time before the Holy Spirit finally completes the cleaning job and enables us to present a clean sheet to the divine scribe.

Abuse, harsh words, ridicule, failure, rejection – the devil's negative graffiti come in many different forms. Sometimes a few words, not intentionally harmful but thoughtless and ill-chosen, can cause a wound that takes years to heal and leaves a scar that never quite fades. How dangerous the tongue is!

It occurred to me recently, though, that in my own life at any rate, there have been correspondingly positive experiences, events, and influences that have counteracted or even replaced some of the negative ones. These heavenly graffiti come in many different forms, often through agents who have no specific Christian connection. They are little gifts from God that may have a disproportionately profound effect.

I can remember two without even trying.

The first happened when I was about five years old and attending the little infants' school in the village of Rusthall, where I was brought up. I was a slightly worried child, not particularly naughty, but given to occasional outbursts when driven into a corner. One day I did something naughty in the playground, halfway through the dinner hour. I can't remember exactly what it was that I did but I do recall feeling that I probably deserved whatever punishment was coming my way. The lady who was on playground duty dragged me into the top classroom and left me there while she reported my crime to the headmistress. When she came back she told me I was to wait on my own until the head sent for me.

I was terrified. My hair stood up and my blood drained down. What tigers there were in this jungle of a world!

At last the headmistress appeared at the classroom door and beckoned me to follow her through the corridor and into her office. I stood facing her as she sat behind her desk. I felt my bowels move ominously. What was going to happen?

After a moment's silence the headmistress pointed to a bowl on her desk and said, "Come and sit down and have some ice cream, Adrian."

She picked up a second bowl, and we sat, side by side eating ice-cream together. She never mentioned my dreadful misdemeanour, and I certainly wasn't going to bring it up. I didn't feel any satisfaction about "getting away with it". I was just puzzled and surprised and relieved to find that authority did not exclude mercy.

The second experience happened just outside Paddington Station in London. I was a raw unsophisticated teenager anxious to project a cool, confident image to the rest of the world. A porter carried my bags from the train, on which I'd travelled, to the bus stop just up the road from the station. As he bent down to put my luggage onto the pavement I felt in my pocket for some change. I knew what to do now. When porters carried your bags for you, you gave them a tip. How much? I didn't know, I'd never been in this position before.

Withdrawing my hand from my pocket I looked at my selection of coins. Airily I selected two florins (a florin was the same as a ten pence piece) and handed them to the porter who was just straightening up. He stood quite still, studying the two coins that lay in the palm of his hand, then, after a searching look into my face, he handed one of them back to me and said in a voice tinged with some mid-European accent, "Two shillings is quite enough".

Even I, naïve as I was, knew how unusual it was for anyone to return any part of a tip. The porter had given me a little free lesson. It warmed my heart to know that his generosity extended to strangers. Perhaps he had a son of my age. . . .

My headmistress and the porter had each offered me, in their own way, the cup of water that Jesus talked about his followers needing. And each will undoubtedly receive the reward that he also mentioned.

Thank God for positive graffiti and those whom he uses to provide them.

Cabbages for the King

IN LOVE WITH
HAYLEY MILLS

Another formative moment. Reading through this again makes me wonder if I wasn't a slightly strange child. What do you think?

I wanted to be an actor.

I bought a book entitled *Teach Yourself Amateur Acting* and studied it in secret, so that when an "opportunity" came I would be ready. My first part would be the lead in a film also starring Hayley Mills, whom I had loved ever since the day when I sat in the delicious darkness of the Essoldo cinema, watching *Whistle down the Wind* three times in a row. It was in connection with my passion for Miss Mills that I learned the second great lesson of my life.

One day, when I was thirteen, I made the fatal mistake of trying to turn fantasy into reality. At that time the Mills family lived a few miles from my home, in a little country village called Cowden. I had often pictured myself accidentally bumping into my beloved in Cowden High Street. It is a fair indication of my naïveté that I saw this romantic encounter developing from the fact that her bicycle tyre had gone flat. Her knight in shining armour would pedal suavely onto the scene, flourishing not a sword, but a pump. She would be overwhelmed by my resourcefulness and subsequently bowled over by my natural charm, which, in my fantasy, was irresistible. Marriage would follow at an appropriate age. Large close-ups, glistening tears, stirring music – the lot!

One day I got tired of pretending. I wanted something real to happen for once. I had never actually been to Cowden, but on this warm, sunny, Saturday morning, I decided that the time had come. I set off on my shiny blue bicycle, tense with excitement, to make my dream come true. My belief in a satisfactory outcome to this expedition lasted for several miles, until the moment when I found myself confronted by a nameplate at the side of the road, which said simply "Cowden". I stopped my bike and, balancing on my left foot, reached over to touch the cold metal of the sign with my hand. It was real. Cowden really did exist. I straightened up again and looked around. Beyond the sign the road continued, bordered by trees, flowers, and bushes. I could see the tops of one or two houses in the distance – Cowden houses. They were all real. Everything was real. By implication, then, Cowden High Street must be real, Hayley Mills must be real. She was a real person, who didn't spend her life hanging around the village street with an incapacitated bicycle, waiting for some scruffy little twit to rescue her with his pump. It was a sad moment. The world was real. As the full absurdity of my daydream dawned on me, I quietly turned my bike around and pedalled grimly back to Rusthall. Another lesson learned – hard but necessary. I would never find what I wanted in fantasy. That frightened me. Where *would* I find what I wanted?

Growing Up Pains of Adrian Plass

EVERYBODY
IS I

It is not a good thing to take any member of your family for granted, but it can happen, sometimes imperceptibly. Every human being is a star in the eyes of God, as I began to learn when I was just ten years old.

It was my earliest encounter with the truth, although I certainly wouldn't have called it a religious experience at the time, and it happened on the top deck of the number 81 bus which used to run between Rusthall and Tunbridge Wells.

The journey only took twelve minutes, but on this occasion that was long enough for a startling new truth to penetrate my ten-year-old consciousness so profoundly that it has affected almost everything I have done since that day. It was connected with something I had read that morning.

As I sat on the front seat of the big green Maidstone and District bus, a sixpenny bit and a penny clutched in my hand ready for the conductor, a phrase I had read earlier repeated itself over and over in my mind.

"Everybody is I."

For some reason, I sensed an important inner core of meaning in the words, but I was unable to dig it out. I was frustrated and fascinated by the problem. If only the answer – the secret, had been a solid thing. I wanted to stretch out my hand and grasp it firmly – make it mine.

"Yes, son?"

So absorbed was I by the intensity of my quest for understanding, that the bus conductor's perfectly reasonable attempt to collect a fare from me seemed an unforgivable intrusion into my privacy. The friendly smile under the shiny-peaked cap wilted in the heat of a ferocious glare from this odd, skinny little boy. The poor man hastily took the two coins from my extended palm, turned the handle on his machine, and handed me a green seven-penny ticket, before returning to more congenial company on the lower deck.

I stared out through the big front windows at the road ahead. We were nearly at Toad Rock. Didn't like Toad Rock very much. Why not? Didn't know really ... Everybody is I ... Everybody is I ... Everybody is I ... Everybody is I ...

We were passing the white frontage of the Swan Hotel now, turning slowly into the lower end of Tunbridge Wells High Street. Good old Tunbridge Wells, like a collection of huge dolls' houses. Lovely day, lots of people about – hundreds of people in fact. Probably going to the fair on the common.

Everybody is ...

Suddenly I stiffened. Body erect, hands flat on the ledge below the window, I pressed my forehead against the glass and stared in amazement at the crowds on the pavement below. The true meaning of those three simple but puzzling words had exploded into my mind, destroying the illusion that I was the centre of the universe, and leaving me to cope, for the rest of my life, with the burden of knowledge. Every one of those people down there in the street, walking the pavements, driving cars, waiting for buses – every single one, whatever they were, whatever they looked like, whatever I thought of them, were as important to themselves as I was to myself! I shook my head, trying to clear it of this incredible notion.

Everybody is I.

That funny, bent old lady with the mouth drooping on one side – she mattered, she was vital – central. The bus conductor who had interrupted my mental churning earlier; he wasn't just a bit player in my world. He was the star in his own. He had a head full of thoughts and feelings; a life inside him; he was the reason that the earth went on turning. My own father and mother, my brothers, aunts, uncles, all my friends – all were "I". Everybody was I, and at that moment I was somehow aware that I would probably never learn a more important lesson.

* ◆ *

Growing Up Pains of Adrian Plass

BACK TO
THE FUTURE

Another Katy story.

Many years ago we took our bicycles down to Newhaven, crossed by ferry to northern France, and spent a few enjoyable days pedalling from town to town along the river valleys. Our last day was set aside to explore the port of Dieppe before recrossing the channel that evening.

Just after lunch we entered the cool interior of a big church near the centre of the town. I lost touch with the others for a while but after a few minutes I discovered Katy, aged four, staring at a life-sized sculpture of Mary, the mother of Jesus, holding her son's dead body in her arms and looking into his face with an expression of real pain and loss. Katy turned to me.

"Daddy, why has Jesus got a hole in his side?"

Stumblingly I explained that a Roman spear had been responsible. Katy was horrified. She studied the sculpture again.

"Daddy, he's got holes in his feet. Why has he got holes in his feet?"

"Look," I pointed to a small crucifix on the wall above us. "They nailed his feet to that piece of wood called a cross, and those are the holes where the nails were."

"Nailed his feet?"

She turned to look at the stone figure again. Her voice broke a little as she spoke.

"Daddy, he's got holes in his hands as well. They didn't nail his hands as well, did they?"

Sadly, I explained. Katy moved closer to the sculpture. She put her arm around Jesus, and rested her face down on his knee.

"Poor Jesus," she said.

Suddenly I longed to go back to the time when I first understood that Jesus died for me and it really hurt, before I covered my faith with words and worries and so-called experience.

◆

Cabbages for the King

THE BODY AND
THE BLOOD

Here is an aspect of my growing-up that continues to directly affect the way in which I understand the nature of Jesus

> When evening had come, and since it was the day of Preparation, that is, the day before the Sabbath, Joseph of Arimathea, a respected member of the council, who was also himself waiting expectantly for the kingdom of God, went boldly to Pilate and asked for the body of Jesus. Then Pilate wondered if he were already dead; and summoning the centurion, he asked him whether he had been dead for some time. When he learned from the centurion that he was dead, he granted the body to Joseph. Then Joseph bought a linen cloth, and taking down the body, wrapped it in the linen cloth, and laid it in a tomb that had been hewn out of the rock. He then rolled a stone against the door of the tomb. Mary Magdalene and Mary the mother of Jesus saw where the body was laid.
>
> Mark 15 : 42 – 47 NRSV

I was brought up for the first twelve or thirteen years of my life in the Roman Catholic church. My mother was a Protestant, but my father's first wife had been a Catholic as well, so there was a sort of RC miscellany distributed in odd corners around the house. There were leather missals, little sacred medals with images of the saints on them, and, distinctly worrying for the kind of small child that I was, coloured pictures of Jesus, looking like a benevolent Swedish hippy, but with his enlarged, bleeding heart exposed, dripping blood down the front of his robe. It puzzled me that he looked so well and unconcerned in these appalling circumstances.

I was too young to take communion at the local Roman Catholic chapel, but I had been told that when the grown-ups went up to kneel down and receive the bread and wine from the priest, these elements actually turned into the real body and blood of Jesus as they descended to the stomach.

Another strange thing I learned was that there were relics – preserved parts of the bodies of important, saintly people, perhaps even Jesus himself – stored in holy places all over the world, and that these bits and pieces could sometimes have a power all of their own in the present day.

There was more than a whiff of the charnel house about all this. I was repelled, but I was also fascinated, and I did manage to grasp one facet of the truth that seemed vitally important then and is perhaps even more important now. It is something about understanding that the physical, touchable, measurable, original body and blood of Jesus are cosmically, eternally important in the spiritual scheme of things. I no longer believe that the bread and wine of communion turn to flesh and blood as they enter my system, but I do know in the very heart of myself that the risen Jesus is not a metaphor, he is a man, who, if he wished, could still come back to earth, stroll along the banks of Galilee, and cook fish for his friends – if he could find some.

This is mystery to the power of a million, but it is not a barren mystery. I have described in another place how much communion means to me. Every time I take the bread and wine there is a rebirth of hope. I pray that the same is true for you.

I suppose this line of thinking was initiated by the idea of Joseph of Arimathea actually coming to grips with the dead body of Jesus. The dormant, long-ago, small almost-Roman Catholic in me suddenly gasped at the idea of this man Joseph having the ultimate relic, the actual body of Jesus, placed into his arms. It was the communion of communions, the body and the blood of Jesus literally given to him, and also for him, and for you, and for me. Three days later the son of

God would rise again from the tomb, just as, when we faithfully receive into ourselves those symbols of bread and wine, he rises in us.

Never Mind the Reversing Ducks

IT'S NOT
YOUR FAULT

Why I Follow Jesus is, unsurprisingly, a book full of reasons why I follow Jesus. One of those reasons is that he is gentle with people who have been badly hurt, and this extract, an account of something that happened in connection with my son, Matthew, is about exactly that.

Let me tell you now about one of the most important things that has ever happened to me. I hope it will mean something special to you, and that through it you might understand more about the compassionate heart of God and, much less importantly, a little more about me.

This experience happened in the early hours of the morning on British Airways flight BA 2028 as it droned through dark European skies from Baku, the capital of Azerbaijan, on its way to Gatwick Airport in England.

I was already feeling quite emotional. Baku was the place where my eldest son, Matthew, was teaching conversational English at a private language school. Sitting on the plane, I was remembering that incredible moment when, on seeing baby Matthew for the first time, I had whispered to myself that this might be the first toy I had ever been given that stood a real chance of not getting broken. Now, just as he was approaching his twenty-fourth birthday, I had spent a week visiting him and exploring a city of intriguing extremes.

Until recently a part of the Soviet Union, Azerbaijan is a Muslim country, shaped – very appropriately considering its geographical position to the east of Turkey – like an eagle flying from west to east. A great oil-producing nation at the turn of the century, it may become so again when the liquid gold begins to flow once more. In the meantime, the Soviets seem to have sucked the country dry and departed, leaving a people who have perhaps lost the will, the way, and the means to achieve a reasonable standard of living. On every road and in every street I saw stalls selling either cheap plastic goods, spare parts for cars, which suffer from the appallingly bad roads, or shoe-mending services, essential because of the equally uneven and unrepaired pavements. On several occasions I came across elderly folk sitting resignedly beside old, dusty domestic weighing machines, presumably hoping that odd passers-by might feel a sudden uncontrollable urge to pay for the privilege of knowing their weight. Some roadside stalls, often but by no means invariably presided over by children, were nothing more than cardboard boxes on which stood two or three bottles of fizzy orange drink of uncertain age. The streets were filled with taxis, mainly Russian-produced Ladas, in such profusion that it was difficult to see who the potential customers might be, other than fellow taxi-drivers whose vehicles had broken down. It had all been rather depressing.

On the other hand, some aspects of Azerbaijani culture were enviable. I came across small children walking home together in the dark with no apparent fear of attack, and all the women I spoke to had that same sense of being safe in most of the streets at any time of day or night. There is no unemployment benefit in Azerbaijan, and the old-age pension is only five pounds per month, but elderly people are not neglected, abandoned, or benignly disposed of. They have a place in their families until death. I found the Azerbaijani people warmly hospitable and more than willing to share the little that they had.

Matthew's apartment, shared with two other teachers, was on the second floor of what must once have been a very palatial private residence. Baku was full of these reminders of a bygone age, splendidly ornate buildings that have been allowed to decay and crumble to the extent that the filthy stairwells and back yards resembled the set of *Oliver*, or those old photographs you sometimes see of poverty-stricken areas of Victorian London. I gathered that there was quite a problem with rats in Baku.

I stayed with Matthew for just under a week, greatly enjoying his company as always and taking a particular pleasure in the experience of seeing him function so well in such a different context. Some aspects of my eldest son's childhood, especially the period when I was ill more than a decade ago, were far from easy for him, so it was good to see the present beginning to eclipse the past. It was hard to leave Matthew when my stay ended, but not at all hard to leave Baku Airport, which must be one of the most depressing places on earth, highly reminiscent as it was of a very low-budget set from the old television series *The Avengers*.

As I sat on the plane, bracing myself for a journey that would last for more than five hours, I thought about the people of Azerbaijan and about Matthew, about the rest of my family, with whom I would soon be reunited, and about the various challenges that awaited me at home. I found myself gradually slipping into an all-too-familiar mood of self-doubt and despair. There are times, and this point of transition was one of them, when faith and hope mean nothing, and all my reference points and benchmarks seem to become insubstantial and float away beyond my grasp. Some of you will know what I mean when I say that I almost shuddered with the complexity and puzzlement of simply being alive and with a deep dread of something in the recesses of my mind that I could not (or would not) name for fear of acknowledging its existence.

Oddly enough, these alarming moments have quite often been the prelude to learning something important from God, perhaps because it's easier to fill an empty vessel than a full one – I don't really know. On this occasion, though, there was no immediate sign of such a lesson, because things started to look up.

It's amazing and faintly depressing, isn't it, to note how the arrival of a meal and a small bottle of wine can temporarily disperse such dark fancies, and I was greatly pleased, in addition, to learn that the in-flight entertainment was to be *Good Will Hunting*, a film which had featured heavily in the Oscar award ceremony for that year. I had really wanted to see that film. Now I was going to. When the video began to play I clamped my headphones to my ears with both hands to cut out extraneous noise and settled down to enjoy a solid hour or two of entertainment.

Good Will Hunting is about Will, a young man who, although gifted to the point of genius in the area of mathematics, is severely handicapped in his practical, personal, and social interactions because of traumatic experiences as a child. The first light of salvation comes through his encounter with an unconventional therapist, played by Robin Williams, who, after a series of sessions in which his patient becomes increasingly accessible, offers him a file containing details of his troubled past and says simply, "It's not your fault". The young man retreats, unable to handle such a proposition, but the therapist persists until, after the fourth or fifth repetition of this phrase, Will breaks down for the first time and weeps on his therapist's shoulder.

I wept as well. Buckets. Quite embarrassing really.

Who did I weep for?

Well, for a start I wept for the children in care I once worked with. I had been through the same process with many of them, saying as clearly as I could, "Some things are undoubtedly your fault, and you must take responsibility for them, but these things, the things over which you had no control, the things which create a whirlwind of fear and anger and guilt in you whenever they rise to the surface of your mind – these are not your fault, and they never were. The time has come to accept that and move on." Sometimes I had even gone through their files with them at bedtime, especially when they were just about to be fostered or adopted. It was a revelation to many of them. At such times I was privileged to witness a lot of bravery and tears.

I wept for Matthew, always deeply loved and cared for but nevertheless with very real demons of his own to exorcise, demons whose presence is certainly not his fault, and I wished I could go back to help him do it, even though he appears to be managing very well on his own.

I wept a little for the people of Azerbaijan, seemingly always being used or abused by someone or other, and especially for the children, who are living through bewildering changes in the historical and political ethos of their country, reckoned to be the third most corrupt in the world. They have so little at the moment, and that lack, and the confusion many must feel, is not their fault.

I even wept a little for myself, and for the rest of my family when their lives are unfairly darkened by the indefinable shadow that has oppressed me since childhood.

Finally, and this is important to me because I believe God wants me to pass it on wherever I go, I wept for so many members of the Christian Church who have been taught only about the anger and retribution and inflexibility of God. I wept for all the men, women, and children who have never really understood that Jesus, the Lord of creation, who justly demands full repentance from all those who wish to come home to the Father, looks with deep compassion on those who struggle to live with wounds from long ago. Laying a hand gently on their shoulder, he says, "I know what they did to you, I know how they hurt you and made you feel guilty and worthless. I know how, over and over again, the past rises in your throat to snatch away the very breath of life, and I also know that it's not your fault. Please hear me say those words to you once more – it's not your fault."

◦ ⬦ ◦

Why I Follow Jesus

POOR
SAD CHILD

My wife and I use this piece when we are reaching out to the damaged child in those we are addressing. It originally appeared in *An Alien at St Wilfred's*, which describes the visit of a cuddly little being called "Nunc" to an ordinary Anglican church.

A: Poor sad child

B: poor child

A: poor boy

B: poor girl

A: don't run, don't run away

B: don't hide

A: we love you

B: we're sorry

A: we let you down

B: we left you

A: we settled for too little

B: we were frightened

A: of your pain

B: pain is better buried, we thought

A: but we were wrong

B: so wrong

A: to leave you there

B: leave you wondering if tears can ever really dry

A: we threw our lot in with the half alive

B: half alive

A: but now

B: now we've come to find you

A: we can face you now

B: we so longed to see your face

A: we want to see you smile

B: see you smile

A: dear child

B: dear child

A: be our child

B: our child again

A: we've brought a friend

B: a friend who changes things

A: he's with us now, his name

B: his name is Jesus

A: Jesus – he can heal you

B: he can make you smile again

A: You'll love him

B: we love him

A: he loves you

B: so much

A: so much

B: so much

A: poor sad child.

•◆•

Adapted from *An Alien at St Wilfred's*

Part Six

DEATH OF LOVED ONES

Losing someone you love is horrible. There's no way round it. You just have to go straight through the middle of the experience and pray that you will come out safely on the other side. Comforting platitudes are of little use at times like these. Joy will come in the morning, but first there is the night.

NEARLY
CRANFIELD

"Nearly Cranfield" is a true story. After forty-three years the memories it evokes can still make me weep.

Nanna is dead. Nanna is dead. Nanna is dead.

This so-called fact beat like a pulse in his brain all through the day and far into the night. They were only words, but they were frighteningly insistent, drumming and drumming and drumming away at the part of him that believed things, until he was almost too weary to resist. He'd known there was something wrong yesterday, on the Friday. Standing in the hall he'd overheard his mother talking in a low, troubled voice to his brother, Simon, on the stairs. He couldn't hear everything she said, but one whole phrase had floated clearly over the banisters: "We all have to be very brave."

He knew what that meant – something dark and horrible had happened. He didn't want to know what it was until his turn came round. There was a special order for being told about things in his family. After his mother and father had talked about whatever it was, it would be Betty's turn to hear next because she was twelve and the oldest child, then Simon, who was nine, and later, assuming that the subject was a suitable one for seven-year-old ears, he would be the last one to know.

He slept as well as ever on the Friday night. Nothing had even remotely happened until he actually knew about it, and he carefully banned guessing – indefinitely.

The air in the house was like thick grey porridge when he got up on Saturday morning. His mother had onion eyes and was too bright. Betty didn't tease him. Simon didn't speak. Dad looked as if he was trying to work out in his mind how to do some job he'd never done before. Dangerous, dangerous feelings rose up from inside him and stopped just before they got to the top. He made them stop. It was like putting off actually being sick till you got to the lavatory. He was good at that. They always said he was a good boy and better than Simon, because Simon just stood in the middle of the room and let it go all over the place and people did extra large sighs because they were sorry for him *and* they'd have to come back in a minute and clear it all up as well. Being sick was funny. He'd always thought it was really your stomach suddenly losing its temper with the last meal you had because it had said something rude, and ordering it out the way it came in with a loud roar. Sometimes . . .

"Christopher, can we go upstairs for a moment? I want to have a little talk with you. Don't bother to put your things in the sink, darling, just come along with me."

Upstairs – that meant it was a very big thing. You only went all the way upstairs for a little talk when it was a *very* big thing. Like when he'd done murals on the new wallpaper for Daddy, and Mummy wouldn't let Daddy talk to him till she had. But this wasn't going to be a telling off, he knew that. It was going to be something sad.

"Can I just go to the toilet first, Mum?" he said at the top of the stairs. "I'll only be a moment."

"'Course you can, sweetheart. I'll be in our room."

He turned the key carefully behind him in the lavatory door. There! He was locked in. If he stayed here for ever and didn't unlock the door again, he'd never hear about the sad thing and then it would never have happened. He sat on the edge of the lavatory and waited.

"Christopher, darling. Hurry up, there's a love."

Mum was calling. He'd have to go. He stood irresolutely for a moment thinking that he'd been in the toilet too long to just do number one and not quite long enough to have done number two. He waited for a few more seconds then rattled the toilet-roll holder loudly and rustled the hanging length of pink tissue between the fingers and thumb of his right hand. Flushing the toilet had always been something he enjoyed. He would do it two or three times every visit if he was allowed. He just did it once now, then unlocked the door and turned to the left towards the bathroom, away from where his mother was waiting in the big bedroom.

"Just washing my hands, Mum," he called.

"Good boy," she responded automatically. "Hurry up though."

He washed his hands as well as he could. If he really had just done number two there would be trillions of germs rushing down the plughole now, choking and gasping on the microscopic mouthfuls of soap that were like poison to them. Remembering to turn the taps off, he gave the inside of the basin a perfunctory wipe and pulled the big yellow towel from the radiator. He dried each hand four times. Four was his special number, and five was first reserve, but was hardly ever used because it got so sulky about having that spiky extra one hanging off at the corner. Four was nice. Settled and square. He loved four.

"My, oh my, nice and dry," he chanted. That was what Nanna always said . . .

Dropping the towel on the floor in a big yellow heap, he shot out of the bathroom and ran along the landing until he was just outside the big bedroom. Shoving his hands into his jeans pockets, he tried to feel ordinary and not unhappy, ready for when his mum had talked to him and it turned out to be nothing very much after all.

When he got into the bedroom his mother was sitting on the far side of the big bed with her back to him, looking out of the window. He stood by the door waggling one leg and hoping that she wouldn't pat the bed and ask him to come and sit beside her. That would be it if she did. That would really be it. He knew it would. Everything would go like a huge soft black quicksand, and he'd sink and sink until he cried.

"What, Mum?"

She laid a hand flat on the eiderdown beside her and smiled over her shoulder at him.

"Come and sit here, love. I want to tell you something."

He jiggered over to her and plonked down on the bed, his hands still stuck in his pockets. He knew he'd got to sit there, but he didn't have to *be* there.

"Can I go an' buy a valve to blow up my football today, Mum? It's been soft for ages."

With a little stab of helpless sympathy, he saw the hurt in his mother's eyes. She thought he cared more about a valve than about her needing him to be her little loving boy. No, Mum! No! I care, I care! I'm here inside and I care!

"Sweetheart, there's something very sad I have to tell you. I've told the others and we're all being as brave as we can."

Not Nanna. Not Nanna. Please, Mummy, don't tell me Nanna's dead. Don't tell me . . .

"I'm afraid Nanna passed away in her sleep last night."

Passed away? Did that mean she'd died?

"What's 'passed away', Mum?"

His mother's eyes were all wet now, and she was shaking her head as if she'd run out of words. He'd done it all wrong. He'd known he was going to do it all wrong. She should have told him while he was standing by the door, then he could have worked up to being nice on his way over to her.

"Does it mean dead, Mum?"

She was crying properly now. She couldn't speak. She just nodded. Then Dad's voice came from the doorway.

"Pop off downstairs now, Chris. Mum's a bit upset. I'll be down in a minute."

"Can I play with the Lego in my room, Dad?"

"Yes, good idea. Off you go."

He listened outside the door for a moment. There was just murmuring at first, then he heard his mother's voice. It sounded hurt and puzzled.

"He didn't seem to react at all. Why didn't he cry or look upset? I don't understand it. He loved her so much."

Back in his bedroom he pulled the big red plastic box from under his bed and started to build a Lego house. He had loads and loads of Lego, given to him for birthdays and Christmas, or for no reason at all, which was usually best because it was a surprise. He decided to make a massive house that no one could break up, using every single tiny little piece of Lego in the box. He would put all the little Lego spacemen and ambulance drivers and firemen and petrol-pump attendants onto the base, and build up the walls around them, then make a roof out of sloping blue pieces so that no one could get out at the top.

He thought about Nanna.

Nanna lived a very exciting half-hour bus journey away in Cranfield. From the top of the bus you could sometimes spot deer in the forest a while before you got to the first houses, and there was a fire station after that, which, if you were lucky, had its big doors open so that you could see the bright red engines inside like two huge toys. Then the bus stopped outside the baker's, but you didn't get off. You waited until you were nearly at the top of the hill that led out of the High Street, then you pressed the red button that rang the bell to tell the driver you wanted the request stop, and the bus stopped right at the top of the hill like a tired old monster, and you got off and you were there. You would feel as if you were crackling like a happy fire as you pulled your mum up the drive towards Nanna's green front door. Then a voice would call out through the letterbox, and it nearly always said the same thing.

"Who's this coming up my front path? Who's this coming to see me?"

Nanna was a bright light with grey hair and a green cardigan, and a spinning top that was old but still hummed, and a box full of wonderful things to make things with, and a drawer full of blown eggs, and a garden with pear trees, and lots of time to read stories, and stone hot-water bottles, and a Bible like a pirate's treasure-chest, and plans for being nice to people that you could help with, and she was the only other person in the whole world, apart from your mum and dad, who you'd take your clothes off in front of, and she was still there living in Cranfield right now, whatever anyone said, and tomorrow he would go there and see her and no one could stop him.

"All right, Chris?"

His dad was standing at the door looking worried.

"Yeah ... D'you like my house I've made, Dad? I'm going to Cranfield tomorrow."

"I like it very much, Chris – it's really great. Better than I can do. There's no point in going to Cranfield, son. You heard what Mum said, didn't you?"

"'Bout Nanna being dead, you mean?"

"Well ... yes – you do know what that means, don't you?"

"Yep."

"What do you think it means?"

"Like Sammy."

His dad squatted down beside him, pleased.

"That's right, Chris, and you loved Sammy very much didn't you? Do you remember what we did when Sammy died?"

"Had a fureneral in the garden."

"Funeral," corrected his dad. "That's right, and that's what'll happen with Nanna as well. Nanna's gone to be with Jesus, so she won't be needing her old body any more. Jesus will give her a new one. Do you understand?"

"Yes."

"But that doesn't mean we don't feel sad about Nanna dying, does it? Because we loved her and we shall miss her very much."

"Can we go to Cranfield tomorrow?"

He could tell his dad didn't want to get angry.

"Chris, have you listened to anything I've said? We're not going anywhere tomorrow, and we all have to be very kind and thoughtful to Mummy because she's very upset."

There was a little pause. He wriggled inside. His dad spoke again.

"You're very upset about Nanna too, aren't you, Chris?"

"Mmmm ..."

He knew it wasn't enough. His dad wouldn't be able to help being a bit angry now. He was standing up and scratching his head and taking deep breaths.

"I just don't understand, Chris. I would have thought – well anyway, do your best to be a good boy and not make things difficult for everybody. Okay?"

"All right, Dad. I *am* going to Cranfield tomorrow, Dad."

That was it.

"All right, Chris. You stay there and talk nonsense to yourself, but I've got too much to do to join in with you, I'm afraid. Just don't get in people's way!"

He'd let Dad make it all okay later on. It wasn't Dad's fault – he just didn't understand.

Saturday went on. Great aunts and rare aunts appeared. They moved heavily from room to room like big brown wardrobes on squeaky castors. He spent much of the day on the stairs. He was only allowed to sit on the even-numbered steps. If he sat on the odd ones he would be taken to a Japanese prisoner-of-war camp and tortured. The fourth one down was the safest. All the steps in Nanna's house were safe. The little squirrel in his stomach was very still whenever he went to Nanna's house. He was going there tomorrow. He was going to Cranfield tomorrow. He was going to see Nanna.

Nanna is dead.

Lying alone in the dark he fought those three words until long after the time when he usually went to sleep. Then, when he did slip into unconsciousness, he had one of the really bad dreams.

This time he was laying a big table for dinner. In his left hand was a basket containing knives, forks, and pudding spoons. He was enjoying himself at first, walking slowly round the table putting a set of cutlery carefully at each place. He took a special pride in making sure that every knife and fork was absolutely straight, and that every dessert spoon pointed the same way. At last, his task complete, he took a step backwards to admire his handiwork. In the process, he happened to glance at the basket still hanging from his left hand. Then the horror began. There was a knife left in the basket. He had left one place without a knife. Terrible, nameless dread seized him as he rushed round the table at crazy, panic-stricken speed, desperately searching for the empty space so that he could put the mistake right before some hideous punishment was inflicted on him. Suddenly he saw the space, and with a little sob of joy, reached into the basket with his hand, only to find that the knife was gone. Then a door smashed open behind him and someone came in. . . .

No one went to church next morning. Dad did the breakfast. Betty took Mum's up on a tray. Simon went off with a friend to play. The air was warm and quiet. A radio was on in the distance. Cars hummed round the corner by their house from time to time. A white dog tapped past on the smooth brick pavement at exactly nine fifty-three. It tapped back again at one minute past ten. He watched everything from the window on the stairs and timed it on his watch with real hands. He'd asked specially for a watch with real hands. He hadn't wanted the other sort. Nanna had said, "Digital, figital, fiddle-dee-dee!" He hadn't been able to say it. They'd laughed. . . .

"I'm off now, Dad."

Dad was looking at the paper, his eyes were dark and tired. He looked up and frowned.

"Off? Off to where? What do you mean?"

"Cranfield. I'm going to Cranfield like I said, Dad."

Dad leaned his head back on his chair and closed his eyes. He spoke in the weak, slow voice that meant he wasn't going to say anything else after he'd finished.

"Chris, you can go to Timbuktu if you wish, for all I care just at the moment. If you want to go and play in the field, then for goodness' sake go! Make sure you're not late for lunch. Be careful. Goodbye."

He could go to Timbuktu if he wished. Timbuktu was in Africa, in the Sahara desert. It was a lot farther away than Cranfield. He decided to believe it was permission. He set off at ten-fifteen, with ten pence in his pocket and his very light blue anorak tied round his waist, to walk to Cranfield.

He knew the first bit very well because it was one of the walks they often did as a family. Turn right at the end of the village, walk straight across the common until he found himself on the black tarmac path, then follow the path until he came up to the very busy main road which had to be crossed if he wanted to get any farther. If in doubt wait until you can't see or hear any traffic at all, then go straight over. He waited for a long time to make absolutely sure, then hurried across. Down the leafy track between the tall green trees, over the big flat car park where the fair came sometimes, down a little hill, and there he was at the place where he and Mummy caught the bus to Nanna's when Daddy didn't come. The next bit was easy too. Round the sharp corner by the sundial church and you were at the bottom of the long steep hill where you first started to get really excited about going to Nanna's. Cranfield was not till you got to the very top of this hill. It might even be a bit farther than that. All you had to do was decide you were going to walk and walk and walk until you got there, and you had to *really* mean it, then it would happen.

He stopped at a little shop halfway up the hill to get some provisions for the rest of the journey. Sweets seemed a good idea because you could get enough with ten pence to make it look like a lot. He pulled one of the little white paper bags from the string where they hung, and filled it with the smallest, cheapest sweets he could find, then took it to the lady at the counter and waited while she added it all up.

"Ten pence, dear, please."

The lady was old and nice. He gave her his ten-pence piece.

"Bye then."

"Bye."

He felt good now that he had a full bag of sweets. Full things had a special, fat, rich feel. He decided that he wouldn't have a sweet until he'd walked another five hundred steps. By then he should be nearly at the top of the hill. If he wasn't, he would wait until he actually touched with his foot the first bit of pavement that was flat. That would make him carry on.

There was a cosy tingle in his stomach as he made these tough plans. He always enjoyed really meaning something.

Five hundred steps later, he wasn't even in sight of the top of the hill. He fixed his eyes on the ground and decided not to look up until he got there.

When he reached the top at last he stopped and lifted his head. The road swept down and away from him, curved up on the opposite side of the valley, and disappeared between fir trees in the far distance. No sign of Cranfield – not yet. It must be farther than he'd thought. Never mind. It was probably just past those trees on top of that other hill in front of him. He'd have one strawberry chew now, and nothing else until he got past those trees and could see what happened on the other side. All you had to do was walk and walk until you got there.

It wasn't just past the trees, and it wasn't on the other side of the big roundabout, and it wasn't at the crossroads after the reservoir (though he did remember seeing that from the bus), and it wasn't at the end of a great long stretch of flat road between fields planted with something unbelievably, startlingly yellow, and it wasn't through a black, echoing railway arch, and it wasn't even just after the forest where, today, there were no deer.

He was running out of sweets. Just walk and walk.

Nanna bought him sweets sometimes.

"Let's put our coats on," she'd say, "and let's tiptoe down to the shops and buy ourselves a little treat."

Sweets or a doughnut. She always let him choose. Then she'd do her real shopping. Shop to shop to shop they'd go, making each different place shine because they were in it being happy. Cranfield sparkled and shone like a Christmas tree because of Nanna. The butcher's shone. The butcher's meat shone. The post office twinkled. The kerb was made of precious grey stone. The houses glowed sweetly. The air had springs in it. Why should Jesus have Nanna all to himself?

He had one small gob-stopper left, and he was nearly there. He knew he was nearly there because he had come to the place where the bus turned right, away from the main road, and Mummy always said, "Get your things together, Chris. We're nearly there."

He turned to the right, took a few steps along the quiet tree-lined avenue, then stopped and sat down on a low wall that bordered a graveyard beside a little dumpy grey church. Opposite him, right on the corner, was a signpost. It told him that Cranfield was only half a mile away. In a very short time he could be walking up Nanna's drive and waiting excitedly for the green door to open and the thin, familiar figure to put her arms out for one of their special cuddles.

The walk home was much worse than going. His legs were beginning to feel like jelly, and his stomach was rumbling and aching with hunger. The gob-stopper hadn't lasted very long, and it wasn't the sort of thing he wanted now anyway. As he trudged doggedly along the way he had come, he dreamed of thick jam sandwiches, meat and potatoes, apple pie and custard, sponge pudding with treacle poured over it, and big blocks of red and white ice cream. It was Sunday, so they would've all had a jolly good dinner while he was away. Chicken probably. He wondered without much feeling whether Dad would smack him when he got back or just shout. Betty would be all big sister, and Simon would be extra nice and good, enjoying Chris being the naughty one. Mum would say, "How could you, Christopher?" and let him off quite soon. He supposed he'd go to school tomorrow as usual. He didn't mind that. He liked school. Especially he liked his teacher, Miss Burrows. Her eyes lit up when he made a particular kind of joke, as though she'd peeped inside his head and knew what was going on in there. Nanna had been like that. Now that Nanna was dead, there was only Miss Burrows (and sometimes Dad when no one else was around) who really knew that funny bit of him.

Funny that he hadn't gone to Cranfield after all, despite being so close. Sitting on that wall he'd suddenly felt cold and scared at the idea of seeing Nanna's house with its eyes shut and all the sparkle gone. He wouldn't have been able to lift the horse's head knocker and drop it again if he'd thought that the hollow, clonking noise had to travel through a sad, empty hall into a sad, empty kitchen where there was no one with flour over her hands who would drop whatever she was doing to come and let him in. He'd always wanted to be allowed to play with lots and lots of flour. He'd like to push his hands into its smooth crumbliness, and move them around underneath the surface, then walk around making white handprints on things and people. What would Mum and Dad say if he asked for a barrel of flour for his next birthday? Three guesses!

Just walk and walk and walk.

How long was it till his birthday? One – no, two months. That was about eight weeks, which was a long time until you suddenly got there and it was now. Dad had promised him a bike. He really, really hoped it wasn't going to be a good-as-new bike. He wanted a brand-new, shiny, perfect bike like the one Simon got last year, only better. There'd been talk of him having Simon's, but he didn't want Simon's. He wanted . . .

He stumbled suddenly as a huge yawn seemed to take all the strength out of his body. He felt so tired now, but he hadn't got the energy to stop. All he could do was walk and walk like a walking robot until he came up against the longest brick wall in the world, or home or something. He noticed in a misty, dreamy sort of way that he was back at the edge of that busy main road that he'd crossed years and years ago this morning. Lots of cars and things roaring to and fro, but somehow he just didn't seem able to stop . . .

"Chris! Christopher! Stop – don't move!"

He stood still, blinking at the frantically gesturing figure on the far side of the road. It was Dad. Dad had come to meet him. Good old Dad. Dad was coming over now. He was bending down and picking him up. It was very nice to be picked up, and Dad didn't seem angry at all. He seemed all soft and quiet and gentle, like someone who's had a big surprise that's made them feel shaky.

"Chrissy – Chris, where on earth have you been? I've been out looking for you for hours and hours. We've all been worried sick."

The jogging motion of being carried was a very sleepy one.

"Been to nearly Cranfield, Dad. Told you I was, didn't I?"

"You told me? Chris, you never . . ."

He could feel his dad remembering.

"You've walked to Cranfield and back, son?"

"Nearly, Dad. Can I have a jam sandwich when we get home, Dad?"

"Sixteen miles, Chris? We never thought ... we told the police you'd gone to the field. Sixteen miles ..."

"Can I, Dad?"

"You can have the whole larder, Chrissy. Mum's still got your dinner on a plate for you. Why did you go?"

"Jus' wanted to – dunno."

They were home. Dad knocked on the back door with his foot. Mum opened it and gave a little cry when she saw who it was. She held her arms out and suddenly he was being held by Mum instead of Dad. She wasn't angry either. She had a big smile on her face and tears were swimming around in her eyes. He'd never noticed how much Mummy looked like Nanna before. She was Nanna's daughter, so it wasn't surprising really. Dad was standing close beside her still. They were both looking down at him.

"He's been to Cranfield," said his dad softly.

"Mum?"

"Yes, my darling?"

"Nanna's dead, isn't she?"

"Yes, sweetheart, she is."

Then he started to cry.

•—◆—•

Nothing but the Truth

WE'LL MEET AGAIN

Part of the joy of heaven will be reunion with people we loved in this life.

My friend Chris loved his mother very much. Widowed relatively early in life, she eventually became unwell and was diagnosed as having an incurable disease. Chris and his wife nursed her through the final stages of what turned out to be a rapidly spreading, wasting disease, until she died in the spare bedroom of their little house in Eastbourne.

It was a complex experience for Chris. The pain of watching his mother's suffering was almost unbearable, especially as she grew thinner and thinner and more and more helpless. Increasingly, he felt as if he was parent in the relationship, and his mother a child, a child whose physical dependency became more pronounced with every week that passed. Occasionally his emotions would overwhelm him and he would sob uncontrollably at the side of the bed, forced into being a child again by the power of his love. At such times his mother was able to reach out an enfeebled hand and comfort him with her touch. Her mind and emotions were perfectly sound and she knew exactly what her son was going through. Through this continual exchange of caring and receiving roles the relationship deepened and sweetened in a way that was quite new to both of them.

Death, when it came, did not seem harsh, and it certainly didn't feel like the end. United on one very important level by their Christian faith, Chris and his mother said their farewells in the sure and certain knowledge that they would meet again, not as parent and child perhaps, but in a new and more complete relationship. Sometime after his mother's death, Chris asked me if I might write something about his feelings and experiences during those last few difficult weeks. The following poem is an inadequate attempt to do just that.

I mothered she who mothered me,
The body that I never knew,
(Though she knew mine so well when I was small and she was all
  my need)
So plaintive now,
Her arms surrendered high to be undressed or dressed,
Like some poor sickly child,
Who sees no shame in helplessness.
And yet, when I collapsed and cried beside her on the bed,
She was my mother once again,
She reached her hand out to the child in me,
She dried my tears
And held me there till I was still.
So ill, so long
Until, at last, when endless days of hopefulness had faded finally
There came a night of harmony, a night of many psalms,
I mothered she who mothered me
And laid my sister gently
In our father's arms.

•◆•

View From a Bouncy Castle

FOOTPRINTS IN
THE BUTTER

Another extract from *Ghosts*. The main character, David Herrick, is describing the immediate effects of losing his wife, Jessica, in her mid-thirties.

In an old schoolboy joke one person says, "How do you know when an elephant's been in your fridge?" The answer is, "You can tell by the footprints in the butter."

Losing someone you have loved and lived with carries echoes of that silly joke. The one who was half of your existence is gone, but, between them, the vastness of her life, and the elephantine, Jurassic creature called death, leave paradoxically tiny marks or footprints all over your house, your heart, and your life. For a long time these marks of passing are to be found everywhere, every day. Each new discovery is capable of triggering a fresh outburst of grief.

Some of them really are in the fridge. On the bottom shelf stands a carton of skimmed milk, one small aspect of the scheme that she devised to make sure of losing a few pounds before going on our planned sunshine holiday in late summer. She bought it on the morning of the day before she was taken ill. The carton should have been thrown out a long time ago, but the dustbin outside my back door is somehow not large or appropriate enough to contain the implications of such an action.

Upstairs, on the table next to her side of the bed sprawls an untidy pile of books that she has been devouring, dipping into, hoping to read. One of them was about pregnancy and childbirth. This was to have been the year . . .

Beside the books stands a tumbler, nearly filled with water.

The books should be returned to the bookcase, but the exact order and positioning of them on the bedside table, the sheer disarray of them, is a unique product of her hands, of her attention and her inattention, and will be lost forever as soon as they are moved or removed.

Her lips were still warm when they touched the cold, hard smoothness of that glass as she sipped from it. The amount of water that remains was precisely determined by the extent of her thirst.

She has no choice now but to give up exactness and inexactness.

These tiny museums of personal randomness are all that is left to me.

How many times and in how many ways is it expected that one should have to say goodbye? I assent and assent and assent and assent to the death of the person I love, yet still she phantoms to life and fades once more to her death in the sad ordinariness of an unfinished packet of cereal, a tube of the wrong-coloured shoe polish, a spare pair of one-armed reading glasses in a drawer, CDs I never would have learned to enjoy, the Bible that is not mine, its thousand pages thickly cropped with markers that were sown over a decade, but have yielded their harvest in another place, her sewing-box filled with "bits and bobs that might be useful one day", familiar doodles on a pad beside the phone, and, buried behind coats hanging in the hall, a wide, dark-blue woollen scarf that, when I bury my face in it, still smells of her.

I disposed of such items as the milk carton eventually. Of course I did. There was never any serious danger that I would descend into some kind of Dickensian preservation mania. The books were returned to their correct position on the shelves. I tipped away the water and washed the invisible prints of Jessica's lips and fingers from the tumbler. It took about half a minute and meant nothing immediately afterwards. I noted how the glass shone and sparkled as I replaced it with its fellows on the top shelf of the cupboard above the draining board. It was, after all, only a glass. Tomorrow I would be unable to identify which one of that set of six had contained the last drink my wife enjoyed in her own home.

In fact, after the very early and most intensely anguished days I became reasonably good at clearing and sorting and dealing with things of this kind as soon as they appeared, albeit sometimes by gritting my teeth or through little bursts of sobbing, conduits that carried away the overflow of continual grief.

The problem was that it never seemed to quite end. Months after Jessica's death I was still having to cope with less frequent but no less unexpected reminders of her life and her death. Some of them came from outside the house, brought by the regular postman, a young man with shiny spiked hair and a brick-red complexion who continued to whistle his way up our front path every morning as if, in some strange way, the world had not stopped turning. He brought letters addressed to Jessica that had important things to say about her mobile phone, or her library books, or which bulbs she might like to order for planting in the autumn, or the amount of credit she had on her British Home Stores card, or the fact that she had come so close to winning eighty-thousand pounds in some magazine draw, that the act of returning the enclosed slip and ordering a year's subscription to the magazine in question was little more than a tedious formality. I answered the ones I needed to and binned the rest.

One or two were innocently cheerful communications from friends or acquaintances from the past who knew nothing of what had happened to Jessica. I replied with as much brevity as politeness would allow, and tried to spend as little time as possible looking at the letters of condolence that followed.

● ◆ ●

Ghosts

GIVING UP LIFE'S
MEMBERSHIP CARD

Ghosts again, and David is taking a walk on the hills with Jenny, one of the old friends that he has not seen for twenty years. Will he be able to properly talk about Jessica's death for the first time?

Morning and breakfast and a change in weather seemed to have cleaned some of last night's darkness out of me as well. I had vivid memories of loving mornings like these, and an unexpected, embryonic hope that it might happen again. Jenny was the only one I had been able to persuade into a morning walk. Coated, booted, and scarved until we looked like two Michelin men, we were planning, with the help of instructions supplied by our hostess, to follow the ridge that ran northward for several miles from a starting point at the top of the hill overlooking Angela's house. The idea was for Jenny and I to join up with the other four to have lunch at a "fantastic" pub called The Old Ox, which, we were assured, was to be found nestling in a fold of the hills just on the eastern edge of a village called Upper Stark.

It had felt strange embarking on this expedition with Jenny. We said all sorts of bright and cheery things to each other as we stepped out energetically up the hill, but there was no escaping the fact that long country walks with women I hardly knew were completely outside any recent experience of mine. My vague discomfort was significantly alleviated by the knowledge that our little capsule of physical closeness involved walking. Like all the best sports and more than a few social activities, walking is essentially a sideways game. Eyes and bodies forward perhaps, but all other important things tentatively sideways – that can work very well. I hoped it would this time.

"Are you going to tell me – any of us – about Jessica?"

Jenny spoke as though she was asking me the price of beans.

"She's gone, Jenny. Jessica is dead. That's probably the first time I've said it so bluntly. She's gone. I know this sounds silly, but when you lose someone you get this nagging, misty idea that if you were to just look hard enough in the right sort of places it must be possible to find them. That's how I felt for a while, but in the end I was forced to face the fact that it wouldn't make any difference how hard I searched for her. Even if I devoted the rest of my life to scouring every last tiny corner of every single country in the world I would never find her because she's dead. There isn't a Jessica to be found any more. I'm not going to see her again because she doesn't exist anywhere."

"Is it too dreadfully crass to make the point that you will be seeing her again in – you know – in heaven?"

I might easily have said the same thing if I had been in Jenny's place, and no doubt I would have regretted it as much as she probably did immediately afterwards. Her words sent me leaping over some cliff-edge of anger that I'd been flirting foolishly with ever since my wife's death. I pressed a hand against my forehead and clenched my teeth as I spoke.

"I don't want to see her in heaven. I want to see her *now*! I don't want her to become something that isn't properly human. Something bright and unphysical and non-confrontational and angelic. I don't want to be met by her in thirty or forty years at the gates of heaven smiling ethereally at me and telling me to come farther in and farther up or anything like that. I have never hated all things mystical as much as I hate them now. I want walks in the wood and having to wash your wellies afterwards. I want trips to the supermarket and arguments over what we're going to do at weekends and underwear hanging in the bathroom and discussions about who could possibly own the origin-less dead-toad shoes that always seemed to collect in our porch and getting into bed together and one of us having to get up again because we've forgotten to lock the back door, and hands and touch and food and clothes and Christmas and talking about people and – and praying together about the future."

A lying pair of magpies flew overhead, pirates looking for plunder on a freezing, foodless day. I lowered my hand and my head, sighing heavily.

"The dead have to give up their membership cards, don't they, Jenny? They can never belong again. Willing or unwilling, they've gone pioneering off to the next stage, changed by the very act of exploration into beings who have no place with us and our weather and our pubs and our feeble attempts to say what we feel. How can they do that to us? How can they?" I smiled bleakly as Jenny spontaneously took my arm and laid her face comfortingly against the sleeve of my coat. "Yes, of course you're right. Jessica has gone to be with Jesus, and thank God for that. Just at the present, though, I can't rid myself of the notion that they've both done a lot better out of the deal than me. . . ."

• ◆ •

Adapted from Ghosts

JENNY

Another Jenny, but this time not a fictional one. This Jenny, the sister of a close friend, took her own life. It is bad enough to lose someone you love through illness or accident, but reactions to suicide can include almost unbearably intense feelings of grief, anger, guilt, and worry. The Jenny in question had been a Christian all her life and had been prayed for continually, especially in connection with the clinical depression that she had suffered from for years. For those left behind there may be agonising questions about whether more could have been done, and about the attitude of God to those who end their own lives. My belief is that God owns people like Jenny as freely and openly and lovingly as he owns anyone else. And so should we.

Our father who art in heaven
Jenny walked in front of a train last night
Hallowed be thy name, thy kingdom come
She was only thirty-seven
Thy will be done on earth, as it is in heaven
You knew what she was going to do, didn't you, Lord?
Give us this day our daily bread
You see, she had no hope left
And forgive us our trespasses as we forgive those who trespass
   against us
Jenny is forgiven, isn't she?
Lead us not into temptation
Lots of us are on the edge of darkness
And deliver us from evil
The only strength we have is yours

For thine is the Kingdom
And she's living there now
The power and the glory
She's yours, Lord
For ever and ever
Jenny
Amen

Cabbages for the King

MY BABY

I have to confess that, as clay goes, I'm not very good at accepting everything the Potter says and does without question. I have often come to a frowning halt while reading Scripture, my twittering finite mind unable to proceed because something God has said or done "isn't fair", or "doesn't make sense". Part of me likes the fact that some questions are unanswerable – one of the best pieces of advice I was ever given was, "learn to live in the mystery" – but another part of me moans and grunts and huffs at the prospect of simply accepting apparently unacceptable truths. God forgives me, irksome though I am, and even, very occasionally, provides aids to acceptance. "My Baby" is one of those.

When I was working on the narration side of a piece about David and Bathsheba, I came to one of those full stops of non-acceptance when I read about the death of David's son, the baby born out of David's illicit union with Bathsheba. The Bible states quite categorically that God caused the baby to fall sick and die as a specific punishment for David's crimes of adultery and murder. I found myself unable to carry on with the narrative because an overwhelming question blocked the way.

Why? Why did God kill the baby? *How* could he?

Traditional answers were no use to me. I knew them – had used them to answer others. They sprang to mind with Pavlovian ease. None of them allowed me to go on writing. David, I was interested to note, was able to accept the death of his child, not without grief, but without a trace of anger or resentment.

I couldn't accept it.

Then, one afternoon, as I was walking the half-mile or so to collect my sons from junior school, a procession of words marched through my brain. When I got home I wrote them down, and soon the narrative was complete. It's not *the* answer. It's *an* answer – my answer, but I think others might find it helpful. One of the devil's most successful deceptions is the one about God standing aloof and detached from human suffering. He knows how it feels, and he shares in it.

I wish you knew how much I love you all. I wish you could trust me in the way that David did. You've asked me a question about the death of a baby. Now I will ask *you* some questions, and you must decide whether I've earned the right to be trusted whatever I do. My questions are about Jesus.

When he was dragged from the garden of Gethsemane after a night of agonised prayer and terrible, lonely fear; when he was put on trial simply for being himself, and beaten, and kicked, and jeered at; did I insist that you solve for me the problem of pain? I let you hurt and abuse my son – my baby.

When he hauled himself, bruised and bleeding, along the road to his own death, knowing that a single word from him would be enough to make me release him from his burden, did I let you down? No, I let you crush him under the weight of your cross. My son – my baby.

And when the first nail smashed into the palm of his hand, and everything in my father's heart wanted to say to those legions of weeping angels, "Go! Fight your way through and rescue him. Bring him back where he belongs," did I abandon you to judgement? No, I let you kill my son – my baby.

And when he had been up on that accursed cross for three long hours, and with every ounce of strength left in his poor suffering body, he screamed at *me*, "Why have you forsaken me?" did I scream back, "I haven't! I haven't! It's all just a nightmare – come back, they aren't worth it!"

No, I loved you too much – far too much to do that. I let your sin cut me off from my son – my baby.

And that death, dismal, depressing and horribly unjust as it was – the death of my innocent son, has brought peace and life to millions who've followed the same Jesus, who came back to life, back to his friends, and back to me.

Trust me. When it comes to the death of babies – believe me – I do know what I'm doing.

◆

Clearing Away the Rubbish

THE DEATH OF
MY FATHER

The news came by telephone one evening, as Bridget and I, married by now, were preparing to take ten of the most difficult boys from the special boarding school where we worked away for a hostelling holiday. My mother said that the cancer that had been diagnosed two years earlier had finally killed my father. I didn't really know how to react, and the holiday, which we decided should go ahead as planned, was actually a rather welcome distraction. The constant activity required in the job I was doing enabled me to postpone the uncomfortable task of looking at my feelings for some time.

When I did finally risk a peep round the wall of my busy-ness, I discovered that I was deeply unhappy. I was unhappy for a specific reason. My father's death had not been unexpected. We had known for some time that his illness was terminal, so whenever I journeyed from Gloucestershire to Tunbridge Wells to visit my parents' home, I made sure that we "got on" well. I felt sorry for him in his diminished, crumpled state, all the old jealousies and insecurities seeming so trivial now that he depended on my mother like a helpless child. Also, if I am honest, I was deliberately trying to put together a reasonable collection of positive memories, ready to pile up like sandbags against the inevitable attack of guilt after his death.

But my immediate unhappiness was not about anything that had happened during his life, but about what was happening now. Had the plump prayer book worked? Had the Roman Catholic Church worked? Had God worked? Where was my father now? I wanted to know the answer to that question more than I wanted anything else. I remembered moments from the distant past when, frustrated beyond measure by the unbridgeable gap between what he was and what his religion said he should be, he had knelt on the floor pounding a chair with his fist and shouting through clenched teeth, "Oh, Christ, help me! Oh, Christ, help me!"

Had Christ heard him, or was it all just a cruel, meaningless game?

By now, my father would know – if there was anything to know – all about heaven and hell. I had only the vaguest notion of what terms like that might mean, but I asked God about it again and again.

"Tell me – please tell me. Where is he?"

I began to think that I would never find peace, until, one night, I had a dream.

There were two parts to the dream. In the first part, I didn't feel as if I was dreaming at all. Perhaps I wasn't. The period just before sleep can be an odd mixture of conscious thought and unbidden, dream-like images. Awake or asleep – it doesn't really matter. I saw the face of Jesus, just above mine, as I lay in my bed in the darkness. It was a face that smiled, and the smile was one that comforted and reassured. It was there for a few seconds, and then it was gone, like a light being turned out. Don't ask me how I knew that it was Jesus' face. I just knew.

The second part of the dream was quite definitely just that – a dream. It began with a muffled knocking sound, someone was knocking on wood with their knuckles, trying to attract attention. Gradually, I became aware that the noise was coming from my left, and, turning slowly in that direction, I saw a coffin. As I stared at the brown wooden container, I knew with the absolute certainty peculiar to dreams, that my father was inside, alive, and anxious to be released from the darkness. With that knowledge came the realisation that someone was standing quietly on my other side, waiting to speak to me. He was a traveller, a man from Tibet, the country I have always associated with hidden knowledge and mysticism. He had travelled a long way, he said, to bring me an important message.

I can hear his words as clearly today as I heard them that night, fourteen years ago.

"There is a rumour that your father has been resurrected."

That was all; the dream ended with those words. In the morning I remembered the details, but it wasn't until later in the day that I connected the dream message with my constant requests to God for information. As soon as that connection was made, I felt peaceful about my father's whereabouts, although I reckoned that at most, I had been given a divine "hint".

This experience is of course a very good example of the kind of incident that can be wrapped in the cotton-wool of spiritual jargon and exhibited from time to time in one's personal museum of "things that show there is a God". Thus, in the past, I might, and probably have, described the events of that night in the following way.

"I was lying awake – absolutely wide awake – when the Lord manifested himself to me, and ministered to me through his spirit in great power, with a mighty blessing. I was then shown a vision as of a coffin, and a great knocking came from within. A messenger of the Lord then appeared, and brought wonderful news that my father was gloriously resurrected. From that moment my soul was at peace, and I knew that my prayers were indeed marvellously answered."

Notice that Tibet has disappeared altogether, and the whole thing is much tidier and more presentable. No, I seemed to see Jesus smiling at me; a man in a dream hinted that my father might be okay; the next day I was no longer troubled; I had been asking God for reassurance. These were the things that happened and they were enough.

•—◆—•

Growing Up Pains of Adrian Plass

POSTHUMOUS CAKE

There are times when the ceremonial and the informal merge together in the strangest ways, as I try to show in this very short short story.

Granny Partington died just before eleven o'clock on a Wednesday morning in the middle of the greyest, drizzliest October there had ever been. She caused as little trouble in her dying as she had done in her living. The little self-contained unit, specially built on to the side of her son's house, was as clean and cosy and friendly as it had been since she first moved in with all her bits and pieces ten years ago. There had been no long, distressing illness, despite the fact that Granny was only a week short of her ninetieth birthday, and all her important papers, including a will that carefully divided three hundred pounds into four legacies of seventy-five pounds each for the children, were neatly bundled and beribboned in the small roll-top desk next to the television.

Rachel Partington had been shopping on that Wednesday morning. She came straight from the car to the annexe with Granny's old cloth bag in one hand and a half-wrecked umbrella clutched optimistically in the other. Coffee with her mother-in-law was not a duty for Rachel. Mum was the only person who accepted her for what she was. They were best friends.

As she stood in the tiny porch, wrestling her umbrella into subjection and flapping out of her son's absurdly large Wellington boots, Rachel chattered happily.

"I got you a *Mail*, Mum, 'cause all the *Expresses* had gone, and I found a really nice bit of beef in the cheap trolley – nothing wrong with it at all. Oh, and you do have to sign the form yourself, they won't let me do it. If you sign it now, Bob can pop it in when he gets home, and . . . Mum?"

No comfortable response noises. No oohs and aahs of warm appreciation and reassurance. No flap of slippers on the kitchen floor. No clink of coffee cups and saucers (Mum couldn't abide mugs). No rush of water into the old tin kettle. No Granny sounds at all.

Rachel found her best friend lying on the bed in her slip, one hand cradling her powdered cheek on the pillow like a child. Later, Rachel wondered why she had been so certain that Mum was dead.

"I just knew," she said to Bob that afternoon, "and I . . . I lay down next to her on the bed for a minute and said goodbye, and cried for a while. It sounds silly, but I wished I'd stayed in the porch for ever, pulling those ridiculous boots off. Oh, Bob, I didn't even have a chance to give Mum her shopping, and it was such a lovely little bit of beef . . ."

Everyone was in for tea that day, but it was a very quiet meal to begin with. They had all heard by then.

Lucy, the youngest, kept staring into the far distance, her four-year-old brows knitted with the effort of understanding what "no more Granny" could possibly mean.

Benjamin was eighteen. He had many strong and radical views, but Granny Partington was not an aspect of life. She was a safe place – a secret repository for his trust in human beings. Inside, he wept like the weather.

The twins, Frank and Dominic, had suspended hostilities as soon as they heard about Granny, both of them crying openly, one at the top of the stairs and one at the bottom, curled up like hamsters with their grief. Frank was still sniffling now, as he sucked orange squash through a plastic straw and ate his beans and sausages. Dominic was white and quiet. He ate and drank nothing. The twins were nearly ten.

Rachel looked across at Bob. He was being very strong and supportive with everyone else, but there was a greyness about his cheeks and mouth that she hadn't seen since Lucy had come so close to dying in hospital three and a half years ago.

Rachel stood up. It was time. "I've got something to show you all," she announced. Reaching into the larder behind her, she took out a jam sponge on a plate and placed it in the middle of the tea-table. "Look," she said, "Granny made a sponge for us. I found it in her cupboard. She'll have made it this morning."

"It must have been the last thing she did." Bob's voice broke very slightly for the first time.

"A posthumous cake," murmured Ben.

"Can we have some?" said Frank.

Rachel sat down, picked up a knife, and began to cut the sponge.

"I'm going to cut it into six pieces," she explained, 'so that we can have one slice each. But no one's allowed to eat a single crumb until they've reminded us of one special thing about Granny."

Silence fell. Six pieces of cake lay untasted on six plates. Granny's sponges were famous in the Partington universe. Like so many cooks of her generation, the old lady had produced these delicious creations by throwing what appeared to be randomly measured handfuls of ingredients into a bowl, stirring them up a bit, then sticking the mixture in an oven. The results were always perfect. This was the last one they would ever eat.

"I know a special thing about Granny," said Frank. "She gave us two pounds on our birthdays, and we always knew it was a lot."

Rachel smiled and nodded. Granny had always put two pound coins in an envelope for each of the children when their birthdays came, and because everyone knew that two pounds was a lot for Granny to give, they treated it as a big and important gift. It was one of the things that had reassured Rachel about her children.

"She was very good at enjoying things, wasn't she?"

"What do you mean, Ben?" asked his father.

"Well, she always thought everything was really nice and sort of sparkly. If you bought her a cup of tea when you were out it wasn't just an ordinary cup of tea, it was a *wonderful* cup of tea. And if you were walking somewhere she noticed all the flowers and the houses and the people. I dunno, she was just good at being happy. Not many people are, are they?"

"Aren't they?" enquired Lucy, who was a very happy child. "I thought they were."

"What do you remember most about Granny, darling?"

"I'm not saying this just because I want to eat my piece of cake, Daddy."

"Of course not, sweetheart," Bob spoke solemnly.

"What I remember most about Granny is her cuddles. She loved me," added Lucy, looking around proudly.

"Her face is like that puff-pastry stuff," mumbled Dominic, unexpectedly. "I squeeze it hard with my hands, and she says 'Go on with you, you'll squash my nose off', and we laugh and she gives me a biscuit." A huge tear rolled out of the little boy's eye and dropped with a plop on to the plate beside his piece of cake.

Rachel put her arm round Dominic's shoulders and rested her face on the top of his head. "The thing I shall always love about Granny," she said, "is that she never made me feel useless and silly, even though I am useless and silly a lot of the time. She made me feel good. I'll miss her so much – we all will." She paused for a moment. "Bob, you haven't said anything."

He stirred and spoke. "I was just thinking – while you were all saying those excellent things – that I've always used Granny as a sort of ruler, a kind of measure, I suppose. Granny loved all of us, but she loved Jesus as well." He stopped and looked at Ben for a moment. "I know some of us aren't quite sure what we think about all that at the moment, and that's all right, but she really loved him and she lived her life the way she believed he wanted her to. Every time I went to a talk or heard a sermon or read a book about what we ought to do or how we ought to feel, I used to think about my old mum. She didn't talk about it much, but she lived it. They won't ever put her in one of those Famous Christian books, but she *was* it. She was *doing* it as well as it could be done, I reckon."

"Can we eat our cake now?"

"'Course we can, Lucy," said Rachel. "We'll all eat our cake now." She looked at the ceiling. "Thanks, Granny."

"Thanks, Granny," echoed everybody except Dominic.

Nobody said anything else until the last mouthful of sponge had been eaten. Then Frank pointed at the plate in the middle of the table.

"There's some little bits left, Dad," he said, his brow furrowed with the effort of trying to remember something important, "aren't you supposed to eat it all up before you wash the plate?"

"You're thinking of something else," said Ben.

"No, he's not," murmured Rachel, as her husband collected the remaining crumbs and put them in his mouth.

• ◆ •

Nothing but the Truth

PLAYGROUND

Another extract from *Learning To Fly*. "Playground" was more enjoyable to write and has been more satisfying to perform than just about anything else I have done. One of the wonderful things about heaven is the fact that having arrived there, those we have loved and lost will be learning what it really means to play.

It seems fashionable to talk about how the previous generation – that graced by myself, I suppose – was wonderfully happy with much simpler toys and activities than those enjoyed by, for instance, my daughter, Katy, who is eight years old as I write.

"Wasn't it lovely," sigh the nostalgists, "when we used to sit on the back doorstep rolling marbles around in cake-tins and that sort of thing? Why, I can remember," they declaim, almost in tears as enthusiasm hopelessly inflates recollection, "an old dead dog we kids used to play with. Now, to the grown-ups around us it may have been something extremely unpleasant, but, my goodness – to us kids that dead dog would be in turn a pirate ship, or a king's palace, or a proper pump-up football, or a scrummy-yummy feast, or a bugle, or a jet aircraft travelling at twice the speed of sound. We used our imaginations, you see? The whole of one summer holiday that old dead dog kept us happy."

You don't think I'm exaggerating, do you?

Anyway, the point I wanted to make was that we would love the chance to have a go on just a few of the things that Kate has enjoyed in the course of her short life. The soft playground is a prime example. Why should children have all the fun?

My friends and I are putting in applications *now* for a bouncy castle, to be permanently available on the lawn at the back of our heavenly mansions. In the meantime, we all need to learn how to play, a very necessary attribute for those who really want to fly. . . .

Oh, God, I'm not anxious to snuff it,
But when the grim reaper reaps me – and me,
We'll try to rely on our vision of Zion,
We know how we want it to be.
As soon as you greet us in Heaven,
And ask what we'd like, we shall say,
"We just want a chance for our spirits to dance,
We want to be able to play".

Tell the angels to build a soft playground,
Designed and equipped just for me – and me,
With a vertical slide that's abnormally wide,
And oceans of green PVC.
There'll be reinforced netting to climb on,
And rubberised floors that will bend,
And no one can die, so we needn't be shy,
If we're tempted to land on a friend.

We'll go mad in the soft, squashy mangle,
And barmy with balls in the swamp,
Coloured and spherical – we'll be hysterical,
We'll have a heavenly romp.
There'll be cushions and punchbags and tyres,
In purple and yellow and red,
And a mushroomy thing that will suddenly sing,
When we kick it or sit on its head.

There'll be fountains of squash and Ribena,
To feed our continual thirst,
And none of that stuff about, "You've had enough",
Surely heavenly bladders won't burst.
We might be too tall for the entrance,

But Lord, throw the rules in the bin,
If we are too large, tell the angel in charge,
To let us bow down and come in.

•—◆—•

Learning To Fly

Part Seven

THE FATHER'S LOVE

Most important of all, naturally, is the fact that we can become members of the family of God if we follow the example of the Prodigal and go home to our heavenly Father. That may sound simple. However, the fact that it is simple doesn't necessarily make it easy, as we shall see.

ADOPTION INTO
HIS FAMILY

I have begun to understand the way in which God is both loving and meticulously demanding, by exploring an image used consistently by Jesus. He knew God as father. Now, as anyone who has read this book so far will know, that image presents problems for me, but there are good fathers around who I have been able to "see in action", as it were, and I have been involved, directly or indirectly, with many children in care who needed to be fostered or adopted by families other than their own. Saint Paul says that Christians are the adopted children of God. God is their new father; so what does a really good father look like?

Joining a new family, adoption into a different kind of environment with different rules and different expectations, needs careful thought and preparation by all concerned. It isn't like joining a club; more a matter of deciding where to put down your deepest roots. The candidate for adoption will need to visit the home in which he has been offered a place so that he can see the head of the household in action, without the pressure of immediate decision or commitment. He will see this prospective father of his being very firm, punishing his children at times. He will see him being very loving and forgiving as well. He might well see him rolling on the floor with the kids, laughing and joking. He will see how he weeps when one of the family is hurt or lost, how everyone is encouraged to love and look after everyone else, and how all have direct access to their father, but show different degrees of trust and confidence depending on what kind of people they are and what their backgrounds have been. He will be intrigued by how different the children of the family are; some quietly, deeply affectionate, others loud and boisterous in the way they show love to their father, a few can manage only a small smile because they hurt too much to do anything else for a while. Some may just sit in the farthest corner of an empty room, paralysed with fear of rejection but nursing the tiniest of tiny hopes that the smile they glimpsed on the face of the man in charge was meant for them as well as everyone else.

They are all in the house. They all belong. The most fearful will be loved into happiness in the end.

If our candidate likes the place, and is happy to take the rough with the smooth, do what he's told when necessary, and accept his adoptive father's control and guidance as a sign of his care, then he'll probably move in. He doesn't have to be perfect, or even good, to qualify, and even after he's arrived, space will be allocated, allowances will be made, time will be spent and given. He'll be left in no doubt about what the house rules are, but everyone will be aware that it takes time to learn and adapt. Adopted children take ages to settle in sometimes. He'll be all right in the end. He might leave, but the offer of a home is forever; he will always be able to come back if he wants to; his new father will never stop loving him, however annoying he may be. Eventually, the spirit of the place will get right inside him; he will mature and learn that he really is wanted. The rules will suddenly seem much easier to keep, in fact they won't seem like rules at all. He will probably be given one or two responsible tasks to perform on behalf of his father. In the end, he will be so well tuned-in to his dad's voice, that a single word will bring him flying to his father's side, saying excitedly, "Yes! What do you want me to do?"

The family image is reinforced for me by what I see in those who really have learned to trust the head of the family. They don't become narrower and more condemnatory, they become broader and more loving. They show little interest in gifts but are profoundly fascinated by the giver. Their spirituality does not seem loony, it feels real; it fits, on some crucial but undefinable level, with everything else that is real. They may be travelling on the hard road that Jesus said was the only road for his followers, but something makes them smile even when their feet hurt. They have usually paid dearly for their joy, and the price seems to be, quite simply, everything. They are convinced that they are the worst of sinners but equally convinced that they are the most forgiven of men.

As far as they are able, they organise their priorities so that God is at the top of the list, knowing that an honest reading of the gospels makes it quite clear that all other things begin from that starting point.

And yet, the effect is not to make someone like me despair and study my sins in a misery of self-loathing, but to feel that the source of all this love and warmth must be able to do something, even with me. I catch sight of God's optimism and feel cheered and encouraged. I remember visiting Peter Ball once with my friend James, whose Christian life has followed an agonised path, not unlike my own. The three of us talked for an hour or so, then, as James and I drove away towards Hailsham, he said with a sort of wistful puzzlement, "He knows a different God to the one I do. His God's nice!"

•—◆—•

Growing Up Pains of Adrian Plass

PRODIGAL
REWRITTEN

Sometimes it is only by inverting Scripture that we recognise the power of the original. Here's the sacred diarist.

Tuesday 15 March

Happened to mention to Gerald this morning that an awful lot of the Christians I meet don't seem to feel they've ever really met God and been properly forgiven by him. You'd think, I said, that Jesus had never told the story of the Prodigal Son. When I got back tonight from a Glander-filled day, he showed me another of these Scripture rewrites of his. Said our chat in the morning had inspired him. Felt quite flattered really.

Oddest feeling is creeping up on me that Gerald is the adult around here, and I'm a sort of earnest adolescent. Quite nice in a way – I think.

At last he cometh to his senses and saith, "All my father's hired workers have more than they can eat, and here am I about to starve! I will arise and go to my father and say, 'Father, I have sinned against heaven and before thee. I am no longer worthy to be called thy son; make me as one of thy hired servants.'"

So he arose and came to his father.

But when he was still a long way off his father seeth him and runneth to him and falleth on his neck and pulleth his hair and smacketh his backside and clumpeth him on the ear and saith, "Where the devil do you think you've been, Scumbag?"

And the prodigal replieth, "Father, I have sinned against heaven and before thee. I am no longer worthy to be called thy son; make me as one of thine hired servants."

The father saith, "Too right I'll make thee as one of my hired servants, Master Dirty-stop-out-inheritance-spending-stinker-pinker-prodigal! I suppose thou believest that thou canst waltz back in here without so much as an by thine leave, and conneth me with thine dramatic little speech? Thinkest thou that this is 'Little House on the Prairie'? Or mayhap thou reckoneth that I was born yestere'en? Oh, no. Third assistant bog-cleaner, unpaid, for thee, mine odorous ex-relative."

Then the prodigal saith dismally unto him, "Oh, right, right – fair enough. So, er, just to get it straight, there existeth no question of lots of nice presents and instant forgiveness and an large celebratory meal involving the fatted calf, or anything of that nature?"

"In thy dreams, son!" replieth the father. "The only gift thou art likely to see is the personalised lavatory-brush with which thou shalt shortly be presented."

And the father taketh the prodigal by that ear which previously he clumpeth, and hauleth him back to the farm.

And lo, the fatted calf beholdeth them approach from an long way off, and, summing up the situation perfectly, throweth an big party. And the fatted calf's family and guests rejoiceth and doeth an bit of disco-dancing, and mooeth sarcastically over the fence at the prodigal as he passeth by in his tribulation.

And behold, as nightfall approacheth, the prodigal's elder brother heareth distant sounds as of an bog-brush being applied, and strolleth out to the edge of the cess-pit after supper holding an large brandy, and he stretcheth luxuriously and picketh his teeth and lighteth an enormous cigar and looketh down and saith, "Evenin', Rambo. I see thou hast returned, then? Likest thou thine rapid progress from affluent to effluent?"

And the prodigal looketh up and saith, "Verily, thou rebukest me justly with thine clever barb. When I had great wealth I shared it not with thee, but now I freely offer thee an good share of what is mine."

And he flicketh at the elder brother with his brush, so that an weighty portion of something exceeding unpleasant ploppeth into his brother's brandy glass, and his brother retireth, threatening to tell on him.

And the prodigal findeth his father and saith unto him, "Behold, all these years during which I was in an far country, mine smug, pie-faced, hypocritical, dipstick of an brother must have caused thee to gnash thine teeth on an daily basis, so how come he getteth all the perks like brandy, cigars, and suchlike, while I remaineth up to mine elbows in other people's poo?"

But his father replieth, "Thine brother is boring but biddable. Get on with thine work, thou less than Baldrick, and think thyself lucky."

The father departeth and the prodigal saith to himself, "Blow this for an game of centurions. I wisheth I hadn't come home now. Behold I am just as hungry, twice as guilty, and four times as smelly. Verily, if, by an miracle, any time off ever presenteth itself, there existeth in my mind no doubt about how I shall seek to occupieth it. Definitely – it's an day-trip to the pigs for me . . ."

Wednesday 16 March

Spent quite a long time today trying to work out whether the sort of thing Gerald wrote yesterday means that he's getting closer to God or further away.

• ◆ •

Sacred Diary of Adrian Plass, Christian Speaker,
Aged Forty-Five and Three Quarters

THE LORRY DRIVER
AND THE ROSE

When you have been given some inkling of the depth of the Father's love, life can never be quite the same again. The following incident happened when I was in my late teens.

It happened when I was hitch-hiking many years ago. I was in the cab of a huge lorry, somewhere on the M4 heading west.

I've always loved hitch-hiking. It's a wonderful blend of adventure and legitimate inactivity. G. K. Chesterton said that he knew few things more satisfying than the experience of being stranded at a railway station. I know what he meant. The flavour of accidental solitude is tastier than Marmite, and I've experienced it most while standing on the side of the road waiting for a lift. I relish the fact that only God and I know where I am. Add to this the knowledge that every lift means contact with an unknown and quite unique human being, and you have the perfect occupation for someone with my twin vices of laziness and curiosity.

On this particular day I'd been dropped off on one of the motorway exits, and I had to wait some time on the corresponding slip road for another lift. It was late afternoon when a very large lorry squealed to a halt beside me. The driver leaned across and pushed the passenger door open.

"You'd better get in, mate. You'll never get a lift standin' there."

I smiled as I hauled myself up to the cab. People said this to me so often, that I quite frequently waited at "impossible" spots, knowing that some kind person would pick me up in the end.

As the huge vehicle rumbled onto the motorway, my new companion and I began the pigeon-holing process that always preceded real conversation. Once he'd established that I was well-spoken, slightly naïve, and not at all threatening, the man behind the wheel leaned towards me and spoke in the tone of one who has made an important decision.

"I'm goin' to tell you somethin' I've never told anyone before!"

He paused, flicking a glance around the cab as though checking for eavesdroppers.

"I wrote this blinkin' poem."

(Actually, *blinkin'* was not the expression he employed. He used a very naughty word.)

He shot a look at me, then went on, apparently reassured by my quiet interest.

"I saw this rose, see? In an blinkin' park. I was just sittin' there, and I looked at this blinkin' rose, and I thought, 'Blink me! Look at that!' So I wrote this poem, didn't I?"

His vulnerability attracted and frightened me. His was a fragile trust.

"Have you recited it to anybody?" I asked.

"You must be jokin'! If I told my mates I'd written a blinkin' poem I'd never 'ear the last of it. Just see me goin' down the local and sayin', 'Oy, I've written a poem about an blinkin' rose.' I don't think so!"

"Could I hear it?"

After some inward struggle he bawled the poem out over the noise of the engine. When he'd finished I said something appreciative, and the journey continued for some time without further conversation.

As I gazed sightlessly through the wide windscreen in front of me, I wondered what God would think about all this. After a few minutes I had to turn my face to the glass beside me. I didn't want the driver to see the tears in my eyes. I felt that I knew what God must think. All the way down the motorway and into the setting sun he probably wept with me for all the people who have poems in them and can't believe that anyone else wants to hear them.

A FATHER KNOWS
NO SADNESS

I've had the same problems with my reaction to starvation in the Third World as most people, I imagine. I find it very difficult to unjumble all the thoughts and feelings that are provoked by pictures of dying children and despairing communities.

"So what?" say some. "Your terrible unjumbling problems are of very little interest to kids who'll be dead next week unless someone does something. Get your wallet out!"

Of course that's true; how can it not be? And yet I can't help feeling that, when it comes to Christians, unless their desire to give arises from a real understanding of and identification with the suffering Christ, then psychological and spiritual gears have a tendency to crunch horribly. The twenty-fifth chapter of Matthew's gospel explains it, and Mother Teresa's words, "He has no hands but our hands" express it perfectly. So did her life.

"A Father Knows No Sadness" fits well to the tune of "O Jesus, I Have Promised", and can simply be sung as a hymn.

A father knows no sadness,
No deeper-searching pain,
Than children who have taken,
But will not give again.
What profit from his loving,
If love is never shared,
What insult to his giving,
If nothing can be spared?
They wait for our remembrance,
The ones who live in need,

The ones our father trusts us
To shelter and to feed.
And if you truly love him,
Then they are precious too,
And if they are a burden,
That burden is for you.

And one day when he asks us,
To say what we have done,
Our answers will go flying
Towards the setting sun.
And how we shall remember
The truth that we were told,
As every word that leaves us
Is burned, or turned to gold.

• ◆ •

Clearing Away the Rubbish

CRY FROM
THE HEART

"If he is my father, and if he really loves me, how can he be letting me go through such terrible suffering?"

A common question, and one that no glib answer will satisfy. This psalmist is asking exactly that question. The little monologue that follows is based on the experience of seeing our youngest son go into hospital for urgent treatment as a very little baby, clearly bewildered by what was going on, and by the fact that we were letting it happen.

O LORD, the God who saves me
    day and night I cry out before you.
May my prayer come before you;
    turn your ear to my cry.

For my soul is full of trouble
    and my life draws near the grave. . . .

You have put me in the lowest pit,
    in the darkest depths.
Your wrath lies heavily upon me;
    you have overwhelmed me with all your waves.

Psalm 88 : 1 – 7

I am less than one year old.

Just now when I was feeling really bad, some people came to my house and carried me outside to a white lorry. My daddy gave me to them even though I felt really, really poorly. He helped them put me in the lorry and then he got in as well. After a lot of bumping we've come to a very big house full of people in white clothes. Daddy left me with a lady who I don't know and she did things to me that I didn't like. Daddy *let* her! Then Daddy came back, but only for a very little while, and he didn't even hold me or look at me because his hands were over his face. Different people keep coming in and staring at me. I'm very hungry but Daddy hasn't brought me any dinner. I feel even more poorly than I did when Daddy gave me to these men. *Why did* he do that?

I don't know what will happen next. I don't like it here and my head feels funny and I don't understand why Daddy doesn't take me home and stop the hurting. Why doesn't he care about me any more? When he comes back in I'm going to cry and cry and cry . . .

•━◆━•

The Unlocking

I DIDN'T HAVE
TO SEE YOU

"I Didn't Have to See You" was born during a period when I was recovering from illness, and it records a growing awareness that the way I feel, physically, emotionally, or spiritually, has nothing to do with any reduction or increase in God's ever-present love and faithfulness. That sounds all very wonderful of course, but I very frequently have a job remembering it. One of his infernal majesty's most effective pieces of rubbish!

I didn't have to see you
In the night-time, there by the side of me.
I knew it had to be you,
Knew you loved the child inside of me.
You smiled in the darkness,
It seemed to blind and burn,
But when my eyes were opened,
I smiled in return, for you were there.

I didn't have to hear you
In the silence, you were a part of me,
I knew that I was near you,
Knew your love was deep in the heart of me,
I knew that you were saying,
Our happiness has grown,
For prayer is only friendship,
You never were alone, for I was there.

I didn't have to hold you,
I was trusting, knowing your care for me,

The secrets I had told you,
Knowing you would always be there for me,
So let the darkness gather,
And let the silence roll,
The love that made you suffer,
Is glowing in my soul, and you are there.

Clearing Away the Rubbish

MY NEW BIKE

We must never forget that God is also Daddy.

I hadn't had a bicycle for years, not one of my own. As a kid I'd had several, including the shiny blue one on which I had set out to find and captivate Hayley Mills back in the sixties. Since my teens, though, I had hardly ridden one at all, apart from an old boneshaker belonging to my friend John Hall, which, I seem to remember, I lost, somewhere in Bromley. Perhaps I thought they were one of the less dignified modes of transport, I don't really know.

Now, in 1985, at the age of thirty-six, my mother was quite convinced that what I really needed was a bike. A nice big bicycle would offer more relaxation and therapy than a hundred books, or a thousand conversations, in her view. I knew better of course. Every time we spoke on the telephone, and she said for the umpteenth time, "Have you got a bike yet?", I would smile indulgently to myself and make vague promises that I *would* get one eventually.

Then, one day as I was glancing through the local advertising journal, I noticed an ad in the "For Sale" section.

Gent's blue bicycle for sale.

Large frame. Very good condition.

Used only six times. £50.

I think it was the "blue" that did it. A shiny blue bike of my very own. The years fell away, and I was an excited teenager again. I'd almost forgotten what innocent excitement felt like. I rang the number at the bottom of the advert, walked round to the bank to draw the money out, and within an hour I was the proud possessor of a large Raleigh bicycle;

not, admittedly, with seventy-five derailleur gears, or however many they have nowadays, but nevertheless a "good bike". How nostalgic the words "Sturmey Archer" seemed as I read them on the gear-lever housing attached to the handlebars. How strange to be back in the world of tyre-levers, cotter pins, saddle bags, chain guards, brake-blocks, and, of course, puncture repair outfits. How satisfying to recapture the feeling of relish when negotiating the narrow gap between the kerb and the lines of cars doing the rush-hour crawl, or waiting for the lights to change.

But most of all I just liked riding around like a kid or enjoying the whiz and swoosh that usually rewarded a bit of grinding uphill work. I had always hated the A-to-Bness of life. Now, I could go where I liked. I could start at A, head for M, and stop off for a while at F if it took my fancy. If I changed my mind at F, then I might forget M and pay a little visit to Q, which, as we all know, is only just down the road from R. It was lovely, and I loved it. I felt about as sophisticated as Pooh Bear on my bike, but I didn't really mind. In the course of just riding easily to and fro, I made real contact with the child inside myself and, in the process learned a simple but profound truth about contact with God. I discovered that prayer didn't have to start at A and end at B either. I learned or started to learn, that it's quite legitimate, and – dare I say – enjoyable, to meander aimlessly around, just enjoying the nearness of God, in the same way that you don't have to arrange special activities in order to enjoy being with a friend or a parent. God sat quite happily on his back doorstep, watching me as I pedalled happily around in my prayers, looking up occasionally to smile at him, and feel reassured by the way in which he smiled back. It was a new experience, and a very pleasant one, despite the occasions when I fell off my metaphorical bike and bawled like a kid with a bruised knee.

●◆●

Growing Up Pains of Adrian Plass

LOOKING BACK

Reading the book of Hosea has taught me so much about the pain in the heart of God. It is the pain of a neglected father.

"When Israel was a child, I loved him, and out of Egypt I called my son. But the more I called Israel, the further they went from me. They sacrificed to the Baals. . . . It was I who taught Ephraim to walk . . . but they did not realize it was I who healed them. I led them with cords of human kindness, with ties of love; I lifted the yoke from their neck and bent down to feed them. . . . How can I give you up, Ephraim? How can I hand you over, Israel? . . . My heart is changed within me; all my compassion is aroused. I will not carry out my fierce anger, nor will I turn and devastate Ephraim. For I am God, and not man – the Holy One among you. I will not come in wrath. They will follow the LORD; he will roar like a lion. When he roars, his children will come trembling from the west. They will come trembling like birds from Egypt, like doves from Assyria. I will settle them in their homes," declares the LORD.

Hosea 11 : 1 – 11

The person who wrote this passage must have been chosen by God because he knew what it was like to have difficult or rebellious children (sorry – that's almost a tautology, isn't it?).

It may be foolish fancy, but I picture God sitting at home in an armchair flicking through old photograph albums in which his rescue of the children of Israel from Egypt is recorded. I've done the same thing myself, sighed and wiped away the beginnings of a tear as those carefully preserved snapshots remind me of when my children were so dependent on Bridget and me for their most basic needs, that there was no question of division or serious conflict between us. We looked after them and they cuddled us – that was more or less the deal. As they get older the loss (temporary though it usually is) of that simple arrangement can come close to breaking a parent's heart. This change in relationship is actually the door to a different but equally profound closeness, as long as we mothers and fathers will walk willingly through the door and close it firmly behind us, but the pain of the process can be unbearable sometimes.

Here is God the Father, then, cooing over the first tottering steps of his little ones, recalling the pleasure with which he healed them, fed them, and removed obstacles from their path, but, at the same time, shaking his head in anguished disbelief over the fact that those same cherished children have now put their trust in other, man-made gods, and forgotten the one who loves them with genuine power and passion.

I don't want to appear disrespectful but, as far as the pain is concerned, he sounds just like me, and I find that rather helpful. If God really does regard me with anything like the same torrential love as I regard my own children (and of course, that's an understatement) then I probably hurt him far more than I have realised when I ignore him and turn to other alien gods who inhabit this little corner of the twentieth century. We are used to the idea of God being angry, but how will we react to the knowledge that he is hurt?

Forgive us if we say
We want to take you in our arms
Sad Father, weeping God
Breathless with the storms
Of anger – of compassion
Fists clenched hard around your grief
Around the marks
The cost
The proof

How can you give us up?
How can you hand us over?
Of course you never can
Never could
Never will
Burdened with perfection and with passion
Lay your head down
Let us hold you for a while
We will try to be to you
What you have been to us so many times
Peace, Lord, be a child once again
Do you remember Mary's arms?
So warm
So different
Rest quietly and soon you will be strong enough
To be a lion thundering from way beyond the east
We will come trembling from the west
We promise you
Like birds
Like doves
Like children who have suddenly remembered
Who taught them how to laugh
But just for now
Forgive us if we say
We want to take you in our arms
Sad Father, weeping God

•—◆—•

When You Walk

I CANNOT MAKE
YOU LOVE ME

A final extract, and one that means a very great deal to me.

====

A couple of years ago I took a six-month break from public speaking of all kinds. The idea was to present my mind to God as a sort of blank sheet of paper. His task, as I envisaged it, was to cover this sheet with a multitude of fascinating spiritual insights that I would then pass on (with suitable humility) to the waiting masses. Forty or fifty of these major revelations would have been quite sufficient, I reckoned – about six in each month.

A rather important flaw in this otherwise faultless scenario was the fact that God was less impressed by it than I was (someone once said that it's easy to make God laugh – you just tell him your plans). After half a year my total score of new insights was precisely "one" – a poor crop from six months of cultivation.

Having said that, this single scrap of understanding turned out to be a very significant one.

GOD CAN BE HURT.

That was all it was, and, to be honest, it was more of a logical conclusion than a spiritual one. How can you love someone, I asked myself, without being vulnerable to rejection or attack by the object of your passion? If this is not the case with God's care for men and women, then his feelings for us are so far away from love, as we understand it, that the term becomes meaningless.

God can indeed be hurt, and a primary cause of such hurt is our failure to respond when he reaches out to us. The grief of God rolls across the face of creation like a deep, sad sea. Omnipotent, omniscient, and omnipresent he may be, but he will never force anyone to love him.

Understanding this deceptively simple fact might increase our buoyancy just a tad.

If I wanted I could take the light
One shining sheet of paper
Crush it in my fist
And then – it would be night
If I was so inclined
I could destroy the day with fire
Warm my hands at all your charred tomorrows
With the smallest movement of my arm
One flicker of my will
Sweep you and all your darkness from the land
But I cannot make you love me
Cannot make you love me
Cannot make you love me
I cannot make you, will not make you, cannot make you love me

If I wanted I could lift the sea
As if it were a turquoise tablecloth
Uncover lost forgotten things
Unwritten history
It would be easy to revive the bones
Of men who never thought to see their homes again
I have revived one shipwrecked man in such a way
The tale of that rescuing, that coming home
Might prove I care for you
But though I can inscribe I LOVE YOU in the sky and on the sea
I cannot make you love me
Cannot make you love me
Cannot make you love me
I cannot make you, will not make you, cannot make you love me

I can be Father, Brother, Shepherd, Friend
The Rock, the Door, the Light, Creator, Son of Man
Emmanuel, Redeemer, Spirit, First and Last, the Lion or the Lamb
I can be Master, Lord, the Way, the Truth, the Wine
Bread or Bridegroom, Son of God, I am, Jehovah
Saviour, Judge, the Cornerstone, the Vine
I can be King of Kings, Deliverer, the Morning Star
Alpha and Omega, Jesus, Rabbi, Carpenter or Morning Dew
Servant, Teacher, Sacrifice, the Rose of Sharon
I can be – I have been – crucified for you
But I cannot make you love me
Cannot make you love me
Cannot make you love me
I cannot make you, will not make you, cannot make you love me

• ◆ •

Learning To Fly

*A major new novel by the best-selling
author of the Sacred Diary Series*

Ghosts

The Story of a Reunion

Adrian Plass

The strangest things happen when friends
are reunited after twenty years apart. When
together last, the friends were members of
the same youth group and – on the whole –
had life to look forward to. Now middle-
aged, some are still optimistic but others are
worn-out and weary. One has lost his faith,
and another is struggling to reconcile the
promises of his Christian beliefs with the
recent death of his wife.

When reunited for a weekend away, the friends find themselves in Headly Manor,
reputed to be one of the most haunted houses in England. What does it mean to stay
in a haunted house? Strangely warm beds on cold days, objects unaccountably moving
from room to room, and little girls in old-fashioned clothes seen walking across the
lawn? Or something more subtle, but potentially much more frightening?

This engaging story blends Adrian Plass's rich style of humour with his knack for
addressing the deep issues we all face, such as faith, grief, love, fear – and most
crippling of all afflictions, the fear of fear.

Softcover: 0-551-03110-7

Pick up a copy today at your favourite bookstore!

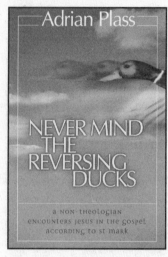

A Fresh, Honest and Humourous
Look at the Gospel of Mark

Never
Mind the
Reversing
Ducks

A Non-Theologian Encounters Jesus
in the Gospel According to St Mark
Adrian Plass

This book is a chatty, quirky, serious, tragic and humourous look at the gospel of Mark. In Adrian Plass's inimitable style, it brings the reader encouraging comment, funny stories, and profound truth. The full text of Mark's gospel is included and is broken into ninety sections. Each portion of Scripture is followed by Adrian's comment and a prayer.

Plass brings his own unique perspective to this meditation on Mark. An adventurous, challenging, witty and often poignant look at the events in the life of Jesus, *Never Mind the Reversing Ducks* addresses the deep issues we all face.

Hardcover: 0-007-13043-0
Softcover: 0-007-13044-9

Pick up a copy at your favourite bookstore!

GRAND RAPIDS, MICHIGAN 49530 USA

WWW.ZONDERVAN.COM

Two Favourite Works by Best-Selling Author Adrian Plass in One Volume

From Growing Up Pains to the Sacred Diary

Nothing Is Wasted
Adrian Plass

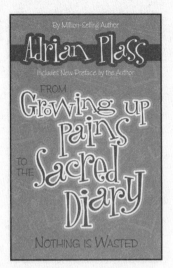

Adrian Plass has a way of telling our stories by telling his, and by so doing has endeared himself to a multitude of readers. Perhaps his secret lies in his humour, from the dark to the absurd. Or it could be his penchant for poking gently but frankly at the foibles of Christian living. Both qualities are on display here, with two of Plass's best-loved books rolled into one.

The Growing Up Pains of Adrian Plass offers reflections on a difficult passage in the author's personal journey, during which the television programme *Company* and some of its memorable guests made a deep impact on Plass's faith. *The Sacred Diary of Adrian Plass Aged 37 1/2* is a laugh-filled, fictional daily chronicle of family and church exploits, featuring Plass's literary alter ego and a memorable cast of supporting characters.

Softcover: 0-310-27857-0

Pick up a copy at your favourite bookstore!

ZONDERVAN™

GRAND RAPIDS, MICHIGAN 49530 USA

WWW.ZONDERVAN.COM

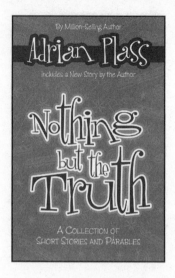

*A Compilation of Adrian Plass's
Best-Loved Stories, Including One
Never Before Published.*

Nothing but the Truth

*A Collection of Short Stories
and Parables*
Adrian Plass

A parable can 'entertain at the front door while the truth slips in through a side window,' and few Christian writers can tell one as deftly as Adrian Plass. In this collection of short stories he is thought-provoking, inventive and easily able to traverse that short distance between a smile and a tear.

Combining material from *Father to the Man* and *The Final Boundary* and introducing a fresh new story, *Nothing but the Truth* reveals the more serious side of Adrian Plass. Seasoned with his trademark humour, the stories portray characters responding to emotional or spiritual crises – and in so doing, reveal truths about ourselves, the games we sometimes play and the love we all are searching for.

Softcover: 0-310-27859-7

Pick up a copy at your favourite bookstore!

GRAND RAPIDS, MICHIGAN 49530 USA

WWW.ZONDERVAN.COM

Three Best-Selling Books – Three Times the Laughter – All in One Delightful Collection

The Sacred Diaries of Adrian, Andromeda & Leonard

Adrian Plass

This book combines three favourites of Adrian Plass's writing: *The Sacred Diary of Adrian Plass Christian Speaker Aged 45 $^3/_4$*, *The Horizontal Epistles of Andromeda Veal* and *The Theatrical Tapes of Leonard Thynn* along with a new preface by Plass.

Best-selling author Adrian Plass takes us on a rollicking tour of his slightly surreal world. From the pungent Andromeda Veal to the loony, loveable Leonard Thynn to Plass's longsuffering wife and irrepressible son, the 'Sacred Diarist' and company are here in full glory, bound for misadventure, loads of fun, and the occasional insight neatly camouflaged as humour.

Softcover: 0-310-27858-9

Pick up a copy at your favourite bookstore!

ZONDERVAN™

GRAND RAPIDS, MICHIGAN 49530 USA

WWW.ZONDERVAN.COM

We want to hear from you. Please send your comments about this book to us in care of zreview@zondervan.com. Thank you.

GRAND RAPIDS, MICHIGAN 49530 USA

WWW.ZONDERVAN.COM